DOUGLAS REEVES

ELEMENTS *of*
GRADING

A Guide to Effective Practice

Solution Tree | Press

a division of
Solution Tree

555 North Morton Street
Bloomington, IN 47404
800.733.6786 (toll free) / 812.336.7700
FAX: 812.336.7790

email: info@solution-tree.com
solution-tree.com

Visit **go.solution-tree.com/assessment** to download the reproducibles in this book.

Printed in the United States of America

14   13   12   4   5

Library of Congress Cataloging-in-Publication Data

Reeves, Douglas B., 1953-
  Elements of grading : a guide to effective practice / Douglas Reeves.
    p. cm.
  ISBN 978-1-935542-12-4 (softbound) -- ISBN 978-1-935542-13-1 (library edition)
  1. Grading and marking (Students)--Handbooks, manuals, etc. I. Title.
  LB3051.R3554 2011
  378.1'98--dc22
                    2010032353

Solution Tree
Jeffrey C. Jones, CEO & President

Solution Tree Press
President: Douglas M. Rife
Publisher: Robert D. Clouse
Vice President of Production: Gretchen Knapp
Managing Production Editor: Caroline Wise
Senior Production Editor: Edward Levy
Proofreader: Elisabeth Abrams
Text Designer: Raven Bongiani

Cover Designer: Pamela Rude

ACKNOWLEDGMENTS

Discussions of grading policies can sometimes be clouded by emotion and unburdened by evidence. I am therefore particularly grateful to scholars who have contributed to the literature on this subject with clarity and rationality. Thomas Guskey, John Hattie, Robert Marzano, and Ken O'Connor deserve far more than a line in a list of references. Their research on the subject of grading and their willingness to engage in public debate about controversial ideas are models of reasoned discourse.

This book is my fourth publishing collaboration with Solution Tree, an exceptional organization that has a greater impact on education each year. Jeff Jones and his entire team provide just the right balance of challenge and encouragement, helping authors to transform ideas into readable prose. Ed Levy shepherded this project through more than the usual set of challenges. He brought order out of chaos, and my ability to complete this manuscript depended upon his patient collaboration.

My colleagues at the Leadership and Learning Center, along with teachers and administrators in schools around the world, give me the opportunity to observe practice and policy, discuss educational and leadership issues, and understand from a practitioner's point of view the elements of grading. It is only because they tolerate my observation and inquiry that I am able to tell their stories. Cathy Shulkin's assistance on research, writing, and the generation of ideas has been an invaluable part of my professional life for more than eight years, and a word of acknowledgment is unequal to the appreciation she is owed.

While I happily share credit with others, the responsibility for errors in these pages remains my own.

—Douglas B. Reeves
Nahant, Massachusetts

Solution Tree Press would like to thank the following reviewers:

Anne Davies
Chief Executive Officer
Classroom Connections,
    International
Courtenay, British Columbia

Lucy Calkins
Professor in Children's Literature,
    Director of the Reading and
    Writing Project
Teachers College of Columbia
    University
New York, New York

Camille Farrington
Research Associate and Assistant
    Professor
School of Social Service
    Administration
University of Chicago
Chicago, Illinois

Thomas R. Guskey
Professor
College of Education
University of Kentucky
Lexington, Kentucky

W. James Popham
Professor Emeritus
University of California at Los
    Angeles
Los Angeles, California

Jennifer Randall
Assistant Professor
Department of Educational Policy,
    Research, and Administration
University of Massachusetts
    Amherst
Amherst, Massachusetts

Margaret H. Small
K–12 Math Curriculum Specialist
Buncombe County Schools
Asheville, North Carolina

Rebecca Woodland
Associate Professor
Department of Educational Policy,
    Research, and Administration
University of Massachusetts
    Amherst
Amherst, Massachusetts

Laurence G. Zoeckler
Assistant Professor
Education Department
Utica College
Utica, New York

Visit **go.solution-tree.com/assessment** to download the reproducibles in this book.

TABLE OF CONTENTS

ABOUT THE AUTHOR

Douglas Reeves, PhD, is founder of the Leadership and Learning Center. He is a frequent keynote speaker for education, business, nonprofit, and government organizations throughout the world. The author of more than twenty books and many articles on leadership and organizational effectiveness, he has twice been selected for the Harvard Distinguished Authors Series. He was named the 2006 Brock International Laureate for his contributions to education. He also received the Distinguished Service Award from the National Association of Secondary School Principals and the Parents' Choice Award for his writing for children and parents.

Douglas edited and contributed to the Solution Tree anthology *Ahead of the Curve* and contributed to the anthologies *On Common Ground, Change Wars,* and *21st Century Skills.*

INTRODUCTION

Whether you are a teacher or administrator, parent or student, policymaker or academic researcher, there are four essential questions to answer on the subject of grading:

1. **How can we make grading systems accurate?** What we ascribe to a student must be not only a matter of judgment but the consequence of evidence and reason.

2. **How can we make grading systems fair?** What we describe as proficient performance must truly be a function of performance, and not gender, ethnicity, or socioeconomic status.

3. **How can we make grading systems specific?** Telling a student he or she is "average" or a "C" does little to help students, parents, and teachers collaborate for improved learning. Students must receive detailed information on their performance so that they use the feedback to improve.

4. **How can we make grading systems timely?** Even if grades are accurate, fair, and specific, students cannot use that feedback to improve performance unless the grades are provided in a timely manner. In this book, we will consider grading practices that meet all of these criteria, and provide practical ways for teachers to save time while providing effective feedback for students.

Accuracy, fairness, specificity, and timeliness—these criteria are at the heart of any discussion of grading. This book considers not only how to answer these four questions, but also how to conduct constructive discussions about grading policy. Perfection is impossible in grading, and therefore our quest is not for an ultimate answer. The goal is not perfect accuracy but a more accurate system; not perfect fairness, but a system that is less subject to bias—both unintentional and deliberate—than was the case before; not absolute specificity, but a feedback system that helps students know what they must do to improve. Finally, while feedback does not always need to be immediate, the prevailing practice in which grades are delivered to students far too late for them to respond is unproductive. Many teachers work very hard to give students detailed feedback, but when that feedback is provided several weeks after the student performance or, worst of all, after the semester has ended, then teachers have wasted their time.

As a teacher, I hope that the ways in which I give feedback will be better forty years after I taught my first class than it was after thirty, but experience has taught me that the only certainty is that I will fall short of perfection. Therefore, I do not offer a simple recipe that readers can adopt with the confidence of certain success. What these pages offer instead are the following:

- A rational process for evaluating the grading systems now in place for your classroom, school, and educational system
- A collegial process for discussing some of the most contentious issues in grading
- A communicative process for bringing all stakeholders— parents, board members, the media, students, union leaders, and policymakers—into the discussion

The importance of good communication about grading policies cannot be overstated. It is not sufficient to be "right"—that is, to have research, logic, and moral certainty on our side of an argument. If our ultimate goal is to improve the accuracy, fairness, and effectiveness of grading systems, then we must not only be right on the merits of an argument but also successful in reasoning with people of different points of view.

Why Is Grading So Important?

For teachers and school administrators, the feedback on student performance that perhaps gains the most attention is the annual exam. In Australia, the United Kingdom, and China, national tests are the coin of the realm, the assessments that mark students, teachers, schools, and entire educational systems as successes or failures. In Canada, provincial examination scores are used to assess students, schools, administrators, and teachers. In the United States, annual state testing determines whether or not a school meets a complex definition of "adequate yearly progress," and it appears that the United States may soon follow a policy of national testing.

Despite all of the political emphasis on annual tests, however, students and parents have a distinctly different focus than school personnel. Their attention is on classroom grades, report cards, and honor rolls. The question parents ask most frequently is not "What was your score on the national exam?" but "How did you get that grade?" Moreover, grades determine academic honors and class rank, and they have a direct impact on college admissions and scholarship opportunities. A 2008 study conducted by Fairfax County Public Schools indicated that 89 percent of colleges responding to a survey use grades to compare applicants, 39 percent of colleges require a minimum grade-point average (GPA) for admissions into honors programs, and 33 percent require a minimum GPA for merit scholarships. More than half of colleges do not recalculate grades based upon the rigor or content of the course. Therefore, the grades that teachers assign can have a profound impact on future opportunities for their students. In addition, the grades that students earn in middle school often influence their eligibility for college-preparatory coursework in high school. Similarly, decisions about which students qualify for advanced courses in middle school are influenced by the grades assigned by elementary school teachers. Grades are also important for both emotional and financial reasons, and it is therefore completely understandable that the topic is sometimes fraught with contention.

Thomas Guskey and Jane Bailey (2001) documented the history of grading controversies for more than a century. In just one system— again, Fairfax County, Virginia—there have been more than half a dozen different grading policies since 1912, with a variety of descriptive, numerical, and letter grading schemes. If we take into account the different systems in use at different schools, then the variation is even greater. The "standard" 100-point scale with 10-point intervals (90–100 = A; 80–89 = B; 70–79 = D; lower than 70 = F) is of relatively recent vintage, dating from the 1960s, and it is now the most widely used system in the United States, according to high schools and colleges responding to the Fairfax survey.

What Influences Grades?

Most teachers, parents, and school administrators assume that the major influence on the grades a student receives is the performance of the individual student. At first glance, such an assumption seems reasonable, but as you will learn in the following pages, a variety of other influences, including the ways that computerized grading systems are programmed, ancient administrative policies, accidental errors, and the idiosyncratic judgment of teachers and administrators determine student grades. If a school system aspires to have a grading system that is accurate, fair, specific, and timely, then it must create grading mechanisms that focus more on the performance of students and less on subjective factors unrelated to student achievement.

Let us begin with the premise that people want to be successful. Students want to learn, teachers want their students to excel, and educational leaders and policymakers make their decisions in pursuit of the best interests of students. Teachers also want their students to arrive in class ready to learn, finish their assigned work, respect teacher feedback, and leave at the end of the year ready to enter the next level of learning with confidence and success. When we assume good will by students, teachers, and leaders, we influence in a positive way even the most difficult discussions. Rather than presume that we must convert bad teachers into barely acceptable ones, let us instead focus on how to help excellent teachers, administrators, board members, students, and parents make better decisions about one of the most important and emotional subjects in education—how to grade for improved student performance.

Of course, grading is only one form of feedback, but it is the form that gets the most attention. Thomas Guskey and Jane Bailey (2001) have argued that feedback other than grading is actually more influential on student learning. This contention makes sense; consider, for example, the encouragement, corrections, and immediate improvements that are the result of effective feedback from coaches and music teachers. However, if a school has an excellent system of feedback but ineffective grading practices, that school will undermine many of its own efforts, and if a school is able to implement effective grading practices, it will reinforce all of its other educational endeavors.

Reconciling Experience and Evidence

We are all victims of experience and context. My overweight uncle lived into his eighties, my pipe-smoking grandmother endured into her nineties, and I know happy and apparently healthy people who have joked that they never waste a single beat of their heart on a treadmill. Of course, this is the same logic employed by adolescents who, because they survived initial experiments with drugs and unsafe driving, believe that they are invulnerable. This is a version of the ancient—and sometimes deadly—falsehood that personal experience is superior to evidence. While students have learned to scoff at medieval superstitions and to value the testing of hypotheses, prevailing discussions in education often remain stubbornly focused on experience instead of evidence.

Casual assertions have a way of becoming accepted with insufficient challenge. Some readers will recall futurists of the 1980s predicting that by the year 2000 schools would be paperless and student writing would give way to dictation into voice-recognition systems. Ten years after the turn of the millennium, neither prediction is close to reality. Today, educators endure similar assertions about their profession and about grading policies. Rhetorical certitude, however, is not a substitute for evidence. When considering how to improve grading policies, one of the most important agreements that teachers, parents, students, and school leaders must reach is that their conclusions will be guided by evidence.

Try this experiment with your own colleagues. Ask them the following questions:

- What enduring principles have you learned in your career? What, in brief, do you "know for sure" about teaching, learning, and student achievement? (If you are in a group, it will be useful to write down all the answers.)

- What beliefs did you have ten years ago that you now know are no longer true? (Write these down as well.)

Compare the quantity of responses to the first question to the quantity of responses to the second. My conjecture is that the first group of responses is extensive. I rarely have difficulty eliciting a conclusion to such statements as "The primary causes of student achievement are . . ." or "The most important components of good teaching are . . ." However, the responses to the second question require some effort. The admission that what we knew a decade ago in education was imprecise, uncertain, or downright wrong appears to require a rare degree of candor.

Now, pose the same questions to an ophthalmologist, climatologist, marine biologist, cardiologist, orthopedic surgeon, or international aid worker. Members of these professions have little difficulty acknowledging that what they know today surpasses what they knew in previous decades. They accept the fact that today's evidence trumps yesterday's experience. A cardiologist knows that twelve years spent in a heart-surgery residency years ago taught her nothing about the powerful effects of behavioral modifications on heart patients.

Thankfully, the use of evidence in medicine and many other fields has led to meaningful and life-saving reforms (McAfee, 2009). However, even in a field that is presumably governed by scientific evidence, practitioners may resist plain fact. Surgeon and author Atul Gawande (2009) describes international evidence that supports the use of checklists in surgical suites and emergency rooms, yet a majority of physicians resist using them. Tellingly, Gawande's survey concluded that more than 90 percent of those same physicians would insist on a checklist if they or a family member were the patient.

This elevation of personal preference over evidence is not unique to education but appears to be part of human nature. We prefer the comfort of the familiar over the discomfort of the new, even if evidence supports the latter. That is why the most rational and reasonable people can do irrational and unreasonable things in resisting change (Deutschman, 2007).

Education in particular—a profession that prides itself on progress—is rooted deeply in past convictions. We lay claim to 21st century learning by placing an electronic board at the front of the class, yet we lecture as if electricity had not yet been invented. We praise collaboration yet assess our students in a manner that punishes and berates peer assistance.

It is not unlike the 19th century, when physicians did not accept the "superstition" of hand washing, even though they knew infant mortality levels were lower when midwives washed their hands before delivering a baby. However clear the evidence, personal experience remains triumphant in too many discussions of educational policy.

How can professional learning communities distinguish experience from evidence? The most effective way I know is to use the following five levels of certainty:

1. **Opinion**—"This is what I believe, and I believe it sincerely."

2. **Experience**—"This is what I have seen based upon my personal observation."

3. **Local evidence**—"This is what I have learned based upon the evidence that includes not only my own experience but the experiences of my friends and colleagues."

4. **Preponderance of evidence**—"This is what we know as a profession based upon the systematic observations of many of our colleagues in many different circumstances in many different locations and at many different times."

5. **Mathematical certainty**—"Two plus two is four, and we really don't need to take a vote on whether that statement is agreeable to everyone."

In a world subject to relativism in every sense—political, moral, and even scientific—mathematical certainty seems elusive, particularly in controversial topics such as educational practices. Nevertheless, there is an appropriate place for the definitive language of mathematics when we approach discussions of grading. For example, when teachers use the arithmetic mean, or average, to calculate a student's grade, they reach a different mathematical result than when they focus on the student's final scores. When teachers use a zero on a 100-point scale, they reach a different mathematical result than when they use the zero on a 4-point scale. These are not matters of conjecture, but calculation.

The first step toward reconciling debate in education, or any other matter of public policy, is for the rhetorical combatants to be intellectually honest about their claims and capable of distinguishing among what they believe, what they see, what they hear from colleagues, and what they have learned from a general examination of the evidence. The problem with the debate over grading, as with every other educational debate, is that we too frequently leap from the first to the fourth level of evidence.

Starting the Conversation About Change

There are two ways to begin a conversation with classroom teachers and building administrators about changing practices. The first is characterized by one-sided enthusiasm. Those zealous advocates who adopt this method typically have good will, good research, and good intentions, but their audiences soon turn from boredom to frustration to active opposition. What began as a collegial conversation focused on questions of practical application ultimately becomes entrenched opposition. Yesterday's reasonable challenge becomes tomorrow's grievance. Thoughtful dialogue and professional conversation are transformed into rancor. Colleagues become opponents, with each side wondering, "Haven't we been down this road before?"

The second way to begin the conversation is with a question, not a statement. Rather than telling teachers and administrators what they need to do, we can ask, "What prevents you from being the very best teacher and administrator you can be?" The following is a sample of the responses to that question that I have heard in the past year:

- "The kids don't care."
- "The parents don't care."
- "Many of the students don't come to school."
- "Students who do come to school are disengaged, inattentive, preoccupied, and angry."
- "Administrators don't support teachers who demand quality student work."
- "Leaders at the system level tolerate poor teachers and administrators."
- "Colleagues won't cooperate and collaborate."

If we were to consider the additional complaints of teachers in rural areas ("I'm expected to teach three different grade levels simultaneously in a variety of subjects") or urban areas ("I'm expected to make up for years of inadequate nutrition, housing, and medical care in a few hours each day"), the list gets even longer. Nevertheless, it is a question worth asking.

This book is not a prescription. Rather, it poses a number of questions and suggests the creation of boundaries. In athletics, each contest has boundaries. No strategy, no matter how creative, is acceptable if it takes place outside those boundaries. Officials, coaches, and athletes know the boundaries of their sport well. Within them are the thrill of victory and the agony of defeat. Outside of them is the zone of irrelevance. This book suggests four essential boundaries:

1. **Grades must be accurate**—The grade must reflect the performance of the student.

2. **Grades must be fair**—The grade must not be influenced by gender, ethnicity, socioeconomic status, political attitudes, or other factors unrelated to academic performance.

3. **Grades must be specific**—A grade is not only an evaluation, but feedback. Students, parents, and teachers must understand not only what the grade is, they must also have sufficiently specific information that they can collaborate to use the teacher's feedback to improve student performance.

4. **Grades must be timely**—While there is, inevitably, a "final" grade that appears on an official transcript, particularly in secondary school, that is but a postscript to a very long letter. Much earlier than the final grade, students should receive a steady stream of feedback, much in the way that students in music and sports receive from coaches feedback that is designed not merely to evaluate their performance but to improve it.

Accuracy, fairness, specificity, and timeliness—those are the criteria for the evaluation of grading polices, and those are the topics we explore in the remaining pages of this book.

We begin in chapter 1 by introducing the concept that grading is not merely an evaluation of student performance but a means to give feedback designed to improve that performance. Chapter 2 frames the main issues in the debate over grading policy and challenges the mathematical distortions that affect many common grading practices. Chapter 3 considers the first criterion, the element of accuracy, and suggests how to improve it. Chapter 4 addresses the element of fairness in grading, focusing on how variations in grading policies distort consistent assessments of student performance. Chapter 5 considers the element of specificity. Chapters 6 and 7 consider the importance of timeliness and offer practical strategies to help teachers allocate their limited time for grading in the most efficient and effective possible manner. Chapter 8 is a discussion of the implementation of grading policies in ways that are most likely to sustain effective change for school improvement.

I hope you enjoy this challenging journey.

Chapter 1

GRADING IS FEEDBACK

Although grading policies can be the subject of deeply held opinions, debates about grading will be more constructive if we first agree on two important premises. First, we should be willing to agree that grading is a form of feedback. Second, we should be willing to agree that feedback is a very powerful instructional technique—some would say the most powerful—when it comes to influencing student achievement.

Evaluating the Evidence

Let's look at the evidence. John Hattie (2009) conducted a meta-analysis of more than eight hundred meta-analyses and evaluated the relative impact of many factors, including family structure, curriculum, teaching practices, and feedback on student achievement. The measurement that Hattie uses is "effect size," or the percentage of a standard deviation in student achievement. Thus, an effect size (the letter d is used to represent this quantity) of .6 means that the relationship between a particular factor and student achievement was 60 percent of one standard deviation. An effect size of 1.0, Hattie suggests, would be blatantly obvious, such as the difference between two people who are 5'3" (160 cm) and 6'0" (183 cm) in height—a difference clearly observable.

Even small effect sizes can be meaningful, particularly if they are devoted to initiatives that save lives. For example, Robert Rosenthal and M. Robin DiMatteo (2001) showed that the effect size of taking a low dose of aspirin in preventing a heart attack was .07—a small fraction of a standard deviation—yet this translated into the result that 34 out of every 1,000 people would be saved from a heart attack by using a low dose of aspirin on a regular basis.

The use of the common statistic, d, helps busy teachers and school administrators evaluate alternative strategies and their impact on achievement compared to variables outside the control of teachers and students. For example, some of Hattie's findings (the value of d follows each factor in parentheses) include the influence on student achievement of the following (Hattie, 2009):

- Preterm birth weight (.54)
- Illness (.23)
- Diet (.12)
- Drug use (.33)
- Exercise (.28)
- Socioeconomic status (.57)
- Family structure (.17)
- Home environment (.57)
- Parental involvement (.51)

These are factors that most teachers would view as outside their control, though some would certainly argue that schools can do a better job of influencing diet, drug use, exercise, and parental involvement. During the eighteen hours every day that students are not in school, students and families make many decisions that influence learning in significant ways, but how important are these decisions compared to the variables that teachers and school administrators can control? The effectiveness of any recommendation regarding teaching and educational leadership depends on the extent to which the professional practices of educators and school leaders have a greater impact on students than factors that are beyond our control. The essential question is, "Is this idea of sufficient impact that it will overcome any negative influences that my students are facing?"

Fortunately, Hattie answers that question with a resounding affirmative response. He found a number of teaching and leadership practices that, measured in the meta-analysis of meta-analyses, are more powerful than personality, home, and demographic factors when considering their impact on student achievement. Examples include teacher-student relationships (.72), professional development (.62), teacher clarity (.75), vocabulary programs (.67), creativity programs (.65), and feedback (.73).

Certainly, Hattie is not the first scholar to recognize the importance of feedback on student achievement. His findings are completely consistent with Robert Marzano's conclusions (2007, 2010) that accurate, specific, and timely feedback is linked to student learning. Thanks to Hattie's research, however, we can now be more precise than ever about how important it is. We can say, based on the preponderance of the evidence from multiple studies in many cultural settings, that feedback is not only more important than most other instructional interventions, it is also more important than socioeconomic status, drug use, nutrition, exercise, anxiety, family structure, and a host of other factors that many people have claimed are overwhelming. Indeed, when it comes to evaluating the relative impact of what teachers and educational leaders do, the combined use of formative evaluation and feedback is the most powerful combination that we have.

If we understand that a grade is not just an evaluation process but one of the most important forms of feedback that students can receive, Hattie's conclusion should elevate the improvement of grading policies to a top priority in every school.

Hattie also encourages a broadly based view of feedback, including feedback not only from teachers to students but also from teachers to their colleagues. We should recall that, as a fundamental ethical principle, no student in a school should be more accountable than the adults, and thus our feedback systems must be as appropriate for teachers and leaders as they are for students. Similarly, our standards for administrators, board members, and policymakers must be at least as rigorous as those we create for fourth graders. If that statement seems astonishing to you, then I would invite you to print out a copy of the fourth-grade academic standards for your location and lay beside them the standards that have been officially endorsed for policymakers, such as legislators or members of Congress. If you can find the latter, you can then decide which are more demanding.

The Evidence-Decision Gap

It is therefore mystifying that a strategy that has so great an impact on student achievement as feedback remains so controversial and inconsistent. It is as if there were evidence that a common consumer practice created an environmental disaster but people ignored it and persisted in the destructive practice. Of course, that is hardly a hypothetical example, as our national habits—such as persistent use of bottled water in plastic containers, dependence upon gas-guzzling cars, and appetite for junk food—illustrate. Rather than embrace the evidence and use filtered tap water, take public transportation, and eat fresh vegetables, we choose alternatives that are less healthy for our families and the planet.

In sum, our greatest challenge is how to transform what we know into action. Indifference to research, though also present in medicine, business, and many other fields (Pfeffer & Sutton, 2006a) is particularly striking in education. An alarming example is the persistent use of retention and corporal punishment. In both cases, decades of evidence suggest that these "treatments" are inversely related to student learning. Retention does not encourage work ethic and student responsibility but only creates older, angrier, and less successful students (Hattie, 2009). Corporal punishment does not improve behavior but legitimizes violence and increases bullying and student misbehavior (American Academy of Pediatrics, 2000). Nevertheless, politicians of all political stripes have excoriated social promotion and urged retention in a display of belligerent indifference to the evidence. More disturbingly, Amnesty International (2008) reports that twenty-four states in the United States, and many other nations, continue to permit corporal punishment, decades after the evidence concluded it was counterproductive. The Pennsylvania legislature continues to debate whether or not to prohibit the practice.

Equipped with a rich literature on the theory and practice of change, educators and school leaders should be fully capable of acknowledging error, evaluating alternatives, testing alternative hypotheses, and drawing conclusions that lead to better results. Instead, decision-making processes are more likely to be guided by personal convictions that are not only antiquated but dangerous. We can be indignant about the physicians of the 19th century who were unwilling to wash their hands, but when the subject turns to educational policies, we sometimes elevate prejudice over evidence.

Before we consider what quality feedback is, let us be clear about what feedback is not. Feedback is not testing.

Distinguishing Feedback From Testing

Consider two classrooms, both burdened by large class sizes and students with a wide range of background knowledge and skill level. The role of the teacher in the first class is to deliver what, as a matter of school-system policy, has been described as a "guaranteed curriculum." Administrators know that the curriculum is delivered because instructional objectives are stated on the board, and the details of the lesson plan supporting those objectives are posted next to the door, where visiting administrators can easily inspect them. In this first class, the most important feedback that students and teachers receive is on the annual test administered every spring. This feedback is very detailed, as it will determine the success and failure not only of the individual student but of the entire school—perhaps the entire school system. Moreover, external companies have established elaborate statistical formulas that will give feedback to every individual teacher, measuring the degree to which that teacher is adding value to each student. When making comparisons of students over three years, these analyses conclude that teachers whose students show gains in test scores have added value to their students, whereas teachers whose students do not make such gains have failed to add value. So ingrained is this sort of analysis that, in the United States, one of the conditions states must meet in order to be competitive for more than $4 billion in federal funds is the commitment to link evaluation of teachers to annual measures in student performance.

There is no question that annual tests are important, if by important we mean that decisions involving the lives of children, teachers, and school administrators, along with billions of taxpayer dollars, will be influenced by those tests. Ask the teacher and students in the first classroom how they know when they are succeeding, and the answer is, uniformly, "We'll know when we get our state test results back."

However, the question at hand is whether these test results really are *feedback*.

Feedback Reconsidered

In her landmark work comparing high- and low-performing nations and high- and low-performing state educational systems, Linda Darling-Hammond (2010) came to an astonishing and counterintuitive conclusion. Since the 1980s, the three exemplars she considers—Singapore, South Korea, and Finland—have made significant progress according to international educational comparisons over the past three decades. More than 90 percent of the students in these countries graduate from high school, and large majorities go to college—"far more than in the much wealthier United States" (p. 192), Darling-Hammond concludes. Detailed field observations reveal the rich, detailed, and nuanced feedback that students and teachers receive daily and can apply immediately.

"Wait," you may ask. "Don't Asian countries like South Korea and Singapore also have a test-focused environment? Aren't those the examples that we tried to emulate to improve our academic performance in math and science?" In fact, this does not comport with the evidence Darling-Hammond (2010) and her team found. These successful nations

> *eliminated examination systems* that had previously tracked students for middle schools and restricted access to high school. Finland and Korea now have no external examinations before the voluntary matriculation exams for college. In addition to the "O" level matriculation examinations, students in Singapore take examinations at the end of primary school (grade 6), which are used to calculate value-added contributions to their learning that are part of the information system about secondary schools. These examinations require extensive written responses and problem solving, and include curriculum-embedded projects and papers that are graded by teachers. (p. 192, italics in original)

Effective educational systems certainly use some system-level examinations, but notice the important distinctions. In these examples, even national examinations include deep involvement by teachers and therefore offer the opportunity for feedback that is far more nuanced than a simple score. Most importantly, the vast majority of feedback is in the daily interactions between students and teachers, not from test scores administered at multiyear intervals. Perhaps the most important consideration is how teachers and students evaluate their own success. While annual high-stakes testing leaves students and teachers wondering about their success ("We'll know how we're doing when we see the scores at the end of the year"), a system characterized by effective feedback offers a dramatically different view.

Darling-Hammond (2010) observed the dramatic difference between the "feedback as testing" model and "feedback as breathing" model, with the latter characterized by feedback integral to the minute-to-minute reality of the classroom. The following words are not from a veteran teacher; nor are they from the graduate of a top-tier teacher preparation program aided by several years of intensive mentoring. They are the words of a prospective teacher who was fortunate enough to see Darling-Hammond's field work but has not yet spent a day in the classroom.

> For me the most valuable thing was the sequencing of the lessons, teaching the lesson, and evaluating what the kids were getting, what the kids weren't getting, and having that be reflected in my next lesson . . . the "teach-assess-teach-assess-teach-assess" process. (Darling-Hammond, 2010, p. 223)

Bridget Hamre of the University of Virginia Curry School of Education notes that "high-quality feedback is where there is a back-and-forth exchange to get a deeper understanding" (Gladwell, 2009, p. 326). Bob Pianta, dean of the Curry School, reported on what a team he led observed in a class with high levels of interactive feedback.

> "So let's see," he began, standing up at the blackboard. "Special right triangles. We're going to do practice with this, just throwing out ideas." He drew two triangles. "Label the length of the side, if you can. If you can't, we'll all do it." He was talking and moving quickly, which Pianta said might be

interpreted as a bad thing, because this was trigonometry. It wasn't easy material. But his energy seemed to infect the class. And all the time he offered the promise of help. If you can't, we'll all do it. In a corner of the room was a student named Ben, who'd evidently missed a few classes. "See what you can remember, Ben," the teacher said. Ben was lost. The teacher quickly went to his side: "I'm going to give you a way to get to it." He made a quick suggestion: "How about that?" Ben went back to work. The teacher slipped over to the student next to Ben, and glanced at her work. "That's all right!" He went to a third student, then a fourth. Two and a half minutes into the lesson—the length of time it took [a] subpar teacher to turn on the computer—he had already laid out the problem, checked in with nearly every student in class, and was back at the blackboard, to take the lesson a step further.

"In a group like this, the standard MO would be: He's at the board, broadcasting to the kids, and he has no idea who knows what he's doing and who doesn't know," Pianta said. "But he's giving individualized feedback. He's off the charts on feedback." Pianta and his team watched in awe. (Gladwell, 2009, pp. 328–29)

The danger in the observation of an exemplary teacher is that we can relegate these experiences to the realm of mystery. Why is he such a great teacher? Some people might conclude that it must be a combination of talent, intuition, mystical insight, and a knack—he just "has it" ("it" being those amazing qualities that all exceptional teachers share). However, we would never say that about a great physician, scientist, attorney, race-car driver, violinist, or basketball star. Indeed, the overwhelming evidence is that talent is not a mystery but something developed with deliberate practice (Colvin, 2008; Ericcson, Charness, Hoffman, & Feltovich, 2006). Can that generalization apply to teaching? Here, too, the evidence demonstrates convincingly that feedback, along with other effective teaching techniques, is a skill that can be observed, applied, practiced, and improved (Lemov, 2010).

The Four Characteristics of Effective Feedback

As we have seen, the clear preponderance of the evidence is not only that feedback is important in influencing student achievement, but also that feedback is relatively more important than almost any other student-based, school-based, or teacher-based variable. It should be noted that evidence on the power of feedback is hardly restricted to the world of education. Dianne Stober and Anthony Grant (2006) and Alan Deutschman (2007) provide evidence from a wide range of environments, including health care, prisoner rehabilitation, recovery from addiction, and education, that depend on feedback. Kerry Patterson, Joseph Grenny, David Maxfield, Ron McMillan, and Al Switzler (2008) add to the body of evidence, using cross-cultural examples in which people were engaged in significant and profound change, even though they could not read or write.

In brief, it is not the provision of a data-driven, decision-making seminar that helps individuals, organizations, or communities change. It is rather the ability to use feedback in clear and consistent ways. However, even the most clear and vivid feedback will be useless if it is not applied with four characteristics: accuracy, fairness, specificity, and timeliness. Each of these is a necessary but insufficient condition for improvement. If information is accurate but not timely, it is unlikely to lead to any improvements. An autopsy, after all, is a marvelously accurate piece of diagnostic work, but it almost never restores the patient to health. Almost every teacher I know labors to be fair, excluding any bias regarding gender or ethnicity in their evaluations of student work, but the pursuit of fairness can impair accuracy. This is particularly true when teachers conflate the attitude and behavior of a student with the quality of his or her work. Feedback that is rapid can be provided by many computer programs, but if it lets a student know only if the performance is correct or incorrect, it yields little information about how to improve the thinking process that led to an incorrect response or how to sustain the analyses that led to a correct one. Specificity is a component of effective feedback, but reams of data delivered months after students have left school are as ineffective as the detailed criticisms written on the high-school English paper mailed to the student weeks after final grades were assigned.

Let's take a closer look at each of these four characteristics.

1. Accuracy

We would all like to think that our feedback is accurate. After all, people with college and graduate degrees know more than their students, so their feedback has to be accurate, doesn't it? In fact, it would be more precise to say that our advanced education has given us *different* knowledge, while feedback must be an accurate reflection of what a student has learned or not yet learned. This distinction— between factual and contextual accuracy— is important not only for classroom teachers but for school leaders and policymakers.

Factual Accuracy

When teaching single-digit addition to first-grade students, the statement "No, Timmy, two plus three is not four; two plus three is five" is factually accurate. However, before we take that for granted, it is worth recalling that many highly regarded tests fail even this basic requirement, as clever students find almost every year that there are either no correct answers or more than one correct answer on high-stakes college admissions examinations. Moreover, student writing is now required on the SAT-R, the Graduate Record Exam, the Law School Admissions Test, and the Graduate Management Admissions Test, just to name a few exams with profound career and financial consequences for each test taker. While great care is taken to provide consistency among two independent scorers or, in some cases, computerized scorers, this level of accuracy is short of being mathematical. According to a mathematical standard, 2 plus 3 equals 5 all the time, while the statement that an essay is worth 4.5 on a 6-point scale is true only to the extent that other scorers agree with that judgment.

This is not meant to suggest that performance assessments, including work involving student writing, speaking, experimentation, and demonstration, are necessarily so subjective that they should not be used. Rather, an appropriate modesty about our professional practices requires that we check the accuracy of our feedback on performance assessments, just as we check the accuracy on a test of single-digit addition. While we cannot have perfect accuracy, we can have a level that is sufficient to lead the student to improved performance.

This leads to the first principle of accurate feedback: a variety of observers, including other teachers, student peers, and the students themselves, must understand the criteria used by the teacher. In the example above, how would you react if a teacher walked into the room and said, "Timmy, if you think that two plus three is four, then that's fine with me, because the most important thing for me is that you love school!" Some readers would, of course, suggest that loving school and mathematical accuracy are not incompatible. In fact, we would express the concern that if children do not learn number operations through a steady diet of feedback, correction, and improved performance, the chance that they will love future schooling in mathematics is very low.

If we are going to require consistent feedback based on well-understood criteria, we should expect the same of every aspect of feedback, including those areas commonly thought to be subjective. Students who have received feedback on a writing assessment know little about the criteria if they can say only, "I got a 2 on my paper." Another student in the same class, using the same scoring rubric, might be able to say:

> I got a 2 on my paper because I left out the three support-ing details I was supposed to put in the second paragraph. Also, my introduction didn't tell the reader very much about what I was going to write next. When my friend Laura read it, she said I should use more power words like "awful" or "horrible" instead of just writing "bad." I think next time I can get a 3 if I work harder.

Note that this is not a problem of specificity—both students had the same rubric. Indeed, in many classrooms today, students are overwhelmed by rubrics. The problem is a more fundamental issue of accuracy—if a student does not know what the rubric means, he or she cannot assess its accuracy. Just as a student can know that "two plus three is five" and not four by engaging in experiments, so can a student know that richer details, compelling introductions, and the use of more vivid language will make for improved writing. Knowledge is not just the result of pronouncements of judgment by the teacher but of understanding by the students.

Contextual Accuracy

Let's return to the original feedback from Timmy's teacher. "Three plus two is not four," said the teacher, with unassailable accuracy. However, while no one would contest the next statement, "Remember, three plus two is five," it does not necessarily meet the standard of contextual accuracy. Contextual accuracy requires that feedback reflect the context of what the student has and has not learned. In this example, how would we respond if the teacher had said, "No, Timmy, two plus three is not four, and remember that standard deviation is the square root of the variance"? The expectation that first graders be able to grasp statistical functions is silly and irrelevant to the lesson. In the same way, we cannot provide feedback that accurately reflects what Timmy has learned and not yet learned until we do some further inquiry. This leads us to another principle: accurate feedback involves asking questions of students, not just making factually accurate statements *to* them.

Questioning

Questioning as a form of feedback is hardly new, as Socrates demonstrated more than two millennia ago. Sometimes it can lead a student to identify a thought process: "Why do you think that is true?" At other times, questions can help a student use another process to test their thinking: "What would the answer be if you used the blocks to find the answer, rather than your pencil and paper?" Similarly, on writing and performance assessments, feedback that consists only of teacher statements ("Unclear sentence . . . Awkward construction . . . Improper usage . . . Another grammatical mistake!") fails the standard of contextual accuracy. For some students, these statements are as impenetrable as a gymnastics score during the Olympics: "The first score is 8.95," says the announcer in hushed tones, "but of course, that's the Bulgarian judge." It's a mystery to me, but perhaps it's absolutely clear to an avid viewer of gymnastic competition. Similarly, members of Garrison Keillor's mythical Professional Organization of English Majors (POEM) may be able to decipher what "awkward construction" means, but most of my students (including more than a few English majors) need some dialogue to sort it out. "Could you please help me better understand this sentence?" is the beginning of a dialogue that can help students distinguish clarity from opacity and replace an awkward expression with one that is more graceful.

While these examples apply to classroom interactions between students and teachers, the principles supporting accurate feedback apply in every context, including feedback provided to teachers and administrators. Whether in the form of annual test results, classroom observations, or formal evaluations, feedback does not meet the fundamental standard of accuracy if the criteria for evaluation are not understood clearly or if they are applied inconsistently. When I discuss with teachers and administrators the value of feedback, they can respond with a weary, "We've already done that," referring to improved practices with rubrics, collaborative scoring, or student conferences, but if I turn the tables and ask about their experience when *they* are on the receiving end of feedback, they quickly dissect the inaccuracies and inconsistencies of the evaluations they received. "I'm the same teacher today I was last year, yet depending on who is making the observation, I'm either superior or in need of improvement. It's a crazy, unfair, and wildly inaccurate system!" So it is, and one of the central purposes of this book is to ensure that we provide students with feedback that is at least as accurate as we provide for the adults in the system.

2. Fairness

My favorite lesson in fairness came from Mr. Freeman French, my junior high school orchestra conductor, who had students audition from behind a curtain. Neither students nor teachers knew the gender, identity, ethnicity, or socioeconomic status of the player. We could only hear the music. While Mr. French's commitment to fairness may seem extreme, it represents a commitment to principle that seems elusive in the context of bias that ranges from Olympic skating to World Cup football where, to put it mildly, fairness is not always the primary value on display. Certainly the blind audition approach of Mr. French had its limits—he ultimately had to look at his performers and give them feedback face to face, but the tone of fairness that he set in his classes conveyed the fact, as well as the impression, that our screeching strings—sharp and flat, too fast or too slow—elicited his feedback solely based upon our work and not our appearance.

I am certain that the vast majority of teachers aspire to be fair, but the distortions in feedback based on gender, ethnicity, and socio-economic status are too consistent and too vast to be explained by performance alone. To take a personal example, in the school where I volunteer, the ratio of girls to boys in the National Honor Society is eight to one; nationally, the ratio is two to one. While the matriarchs in my life may have persuaded me that women are smarter than men, they have yet to persuade me that their gender is eight times, or even two times, as smart as mine. Similarly, the relationship between socio-economic and ethnic variables and student test scores is consistent and pervasive (Herrnstein & Murray, 1994), but those relationships say more about how popular tests value what wealthy white kids know than they do about the intellectual incapacity of poor minority kids.

Unfortunately, the cure for unfairness in standardized tests can be worse than the disease, if teachers seek to compensate for unfairness by awarding high grades for poor performance. The pursuit of fairness at the expense of accuracy and specificity does not advance the cause of equity.

3. Specificity

The third criterion for effective feedback is that it must be specific. There is a long-running dispute among assessment writers about the use of different sorts of rubrics and the relative merits of holistic and analytic rubrics. Grant Wiggins (1998) explains that a holistic rubric "yields a single score based on an overall impression" (p. 164). By contrast, an analytic rubric "isolates each major trait into a separate rubric with its own criteria" (p. 164). The essential principle, however, is not the label of the rubric but the degree to which it is applied consistently. Therefore, when we use rubrics that contain terms like *little evidence* followed by *some evidence, sufficient evidence,* and *superior evidence*, we are inviting chaotic ambiguity.

The Perils of Specificity

The antidote to ambiguity is not micromanagement. Students, administrators, and teachers have all uttered those words signaling the surrender of independent thought, "Just tell me what to do," when they have been frustrated by directions that were too ambiguous. Hard work and collaborative effort, when accompanied by failures in mind-reading, can lead to disappointing results. Certainly, hyper-explicit instruction is tempting. When we are clear in our requirements, students, teachers, and leaders can do exactly what is required, neither more nor less. Students will produce essays with precisely five paragraphs—never more parsimoniously or extravagantly detailed than the formula suggests. Teachers will print lesson plans precisely as prescribed and write state standards and learning objectives on the board. School administrators will create strategic plans that conform to the format and style required by higher authorities. However, when feedback is too specific, students are assessed only on the extent to which they can follow a formula, not engage in learning. Telltale signs that well-intended rubrics have been subverted into mindless formulas include student work that almost uniformly begins with the same sentence.

How can teachers reach a balance between feedback that is too specific and feedback that is too ambiguous? Two principles, pulling in different directions, help teachers strive for this balance. The first concerns boundaries and our interpretations of them, and the second concerns consistency.

Boundaries, Judgment Calls, and Creativity

There are one hundred yards from one end of a football field to the other, not including the two end zones, and each team is allowed to place eleven players on the field, provided that the players remain on their own side of an imaginary line—the line of scrimmage. These boundaries are explicit and unchanging. The decision about where to place the players within them, however, is a judgment call. Similarly, fixed boundaries for classroom feedback include spelling and mathematical accuracy, but whether *egregious* should be substituted for *terrible* or whether bar charts should be oriented vertically or horizontally is a judgment call.

For the past five years, I have served as the volunteer coach of a local high school debate team. Students have explicit boundaries, including time limits for speeches, the resolution that must be debated, and the integrity of the evidence that they use during the competition. This experience serves as a useful illustration for the essential balance between explicit and flexible feedback on student performance. Applying excessively rigid boundaries for students may unintentionally lead them to become parrots instead of debaters, mimicking the arguments and evidence that they find on commercial websites that cater to affluent schools and students. Thus, the judge of these unfortunate students will listen to the same speeches, same arguments, and even the same grammatical errors, round after round, tournament after tournament. The students read the computer print-outs, with their intensity interrupted only by the sound of the timer indicating that their time has expired.

If their competitors are locked into the same trap of specificity, then they might respond not with a refutation of the arguments presented by their opponents but with another commercially prepared speech, the reading of which is also interrupted only by the timer. These exchanges are not illuminating for the judge, the competitors, or the audience, and therefore these debates represent the opposite of the critical thinking and rhetorical engagement that the activity might have offered to them.

An opposite but equally pernicious trend has recently emerged. Labeled the "critique" by debate theorists (Hensley & Carlin, 2005), these students argue that debate resolutions are artificial boundaries and that they should be free to address issues of greater importance to society. We will overlook, at least in this context, the fact that these students and their coaches embrace without a hint of irony rules about time limits, ballots, speaker points, and, most especially, trophies. It is not that they truly want the absence of rules, but rather they want to select the rules that will be most familiar to them and least familiar to their opponent. It is as if one side of an athletic competition rolled onto the field equipped with tanks rather than shoulder pads but insisted that the time limits and boundaries of the playing field remain the same.

Where is the middle ground? In the classroom, as in other endeavors, there is a blend of specificity and creativity. Within a single debate resolution, students can think of hundreds of arguments. Within the rules of football, there are thousands of different offensive and defensive formations. One reason I enjoy watching cricket is the seemingly infinite variety of ways that players can respond to a unique combination of batsman and bowler. There is, in brief, a balance between boundaries and freedom, and that is not only a key to effective feedback but to surviving in a free society.

Consistency

Second, expect consistency about boundaries but variation in student performance within them—a direct result of variation in judgment calls. How consistent is good enough? Feedback that is sufficiently specific should be consistent 80 percent or more of the time. Why is 80 percent important rather than 50 or 90 percent? When psychometricians, experts on measurement and testing, evaluate high-stakes tests, they use the term *reliability* to assess the consistency of the test. They expect that students who answer a test item correctly to answer similar items correctly. Reliability is never perfect, but in general, the more consistent a test, the more reliable it is deemed to be. As a practical matter, testing experts generally expect about 80 percent consistency (a reliability coefficient of .80) on tests for them to be deemed acceptably reliable. That is why classroom feedback should be similarly consistent; about four out of five teachers who look at a piece of student work should agree that it is proficient or not proficient. The more specific the feedback guidelines are, the more consistent—the more reliable—the feedback will be.

Let's apply this theory in practical terms in the classroom. If five sources—three peers, a teacher, and a student doing a self-assessment—provide feedback on student work, four of those five sources should be consistent. That is, the feedback will include the same score on the rubric and very similar suggestions for improvement. This standard allows for some differences—peer feedback can be influenced by interpersonal relationships, and some students can be hypercritical of their own work—but if a student is not receiving consistent feedback, then the culprit may well be ambiguous qualifiers, such as "sometimes," "sufficient," "adequate," or "good," which invite different feedback on the same work.

4. Timeliness

When we say that feedback is timely, we mean that students receive the feedback with sufficient promptness to influence their performance. In most sports, electronic games, and music rehearsals feedback is virtually instantaneous—the bad play, wrong maneuver, and sour note are all met with immediate feedback that leads students to stop and improve their performance. When conducting a science lab, solving a complex equation, or writing a paper, however, the length of time separating performance from feedback may be longer.

In the context of student work, the extent to which we meet the standard of timeliness is a function of the degree to which it can be and is used by the student. For example, Lucy Calkins, founder of the Teachers College Reading and Writing Project at Columbia University, pioneered a process in which students receive feedback from peers, teachers, and systematic self-assessment in order to improve the quality of their writing. Her rich illustrations of the value of feedback (Calkins, 1983, 1994) demonstrate that the difference between poor writing and that attributed to a "gifted" child is not the background of the child or the identity of the teacher but the quality, consistency, and frequency of the feedback. I've watched Professor Calkins present these examples in small seminars and in large audiences of more than two thousand teachers, but despite changes in the learning environment, the insight by the participating teachers is invariably the same: they can't believe that the different writing samples are from the same children. The children were the same; what changed is the quality of the feedback.

The greater the number of students, the more challenging it is for teachers to provide timely feedback. To do this in secondary schools, where a teacher may have five different classes with thirty or more students each—more than one hundred fifty in all—is a particular challenge for teachers. It is not, however, impossible. At Harlem Village Academy, a school with 100 percent poor and minority students, where all of them passed the New York Regents examination, students routinely give one another feedback on everything from math problem solving to hallway behavior.

Self-assessment can also be a rich source of timely feedback, provided that students are able to engage in an objective comparison of their work to a clear standard. An environment of consistent and timely feedback offers multiple benefits for a school, and it is the opposite of a system in which the only person qualified to provide feedback is the one holding the red pencil, the grade book, or the bullhorn. The essential principle for timely feedback is that students have multiple sources of information, including a clear and consistent system of peer assessment and self-assessment.

Choosing the Time

While the use of scoring rubrics has certainly been a positive step forward in the past few decades, there remains wide variation in the quality, consistency, and clarity of these instruments, particularly if they are to be used quickly and accurately by students. Larry Ainsworth and Jan Christinson's (1998) *Student-Generated Rubrics* is a useful beginning, but the ultimate test of the quality of the rubric is not the words on the scoring rubric itself but the impact that it has on student work. For example, I have created what I thought were stunningly clear rubrics for my students, only to find that in their second drafts, they made the same errors—perhaps a bit more neatly—as they did in their first. In other words, a well-crafted rubric met with uncomprehending compliance by students will fail to deliver timely feedback. Therefore, while the expert who crafts a rubric may wish to include many elements, it is necessary to provide *just enough feedback at the time it can be used* for improved performance.

Effective athletic coaches are masterful at this, as are the most effective orchestral and choral conductors. While ineffective coaches hurl an unending stream of criticism and directions from the sidelines to their bewildered players, the best coaches give direction in a way that will influence the action at precisely the right time. It is interesting to watch how two of the great symphonic conductors of our time, James Levine and Lorin Maazel, move so little, even during rehearsals. Their feedback is precisely at the point in the music when it has the maximum impact. On the best athletic teams and in symphony orchestras, there is an exquisite network of communication—the alert from a fellow player, the arched bow, the lifted head—all of which reinforce and support the feedback from the coach or conductor.

Table 1.1 summarizes techniques to apply for ensuring accurate, fair, specific, and timely feedback.

Table 1.1: Elements of Effective Feedback

Elements of Effective Feedback	Techniques for Effective Feedback
Accurate	Different observers, including other teachers, student peers, and the students themselves, understand the criteria used by the teacher to provide feedback.
	Teachers do not just make factually accurate statements to students; they ask students questions.
Fair	Feedback is not influenced by the gender, ethnicity, socioeconomic status, or other characteristics of the students.
	Teachers do not seek to compensate for biases in other tests by displaying reverse bias or awarding higher grades for lower performances by disadvantaged students.
Specific	Boundaries are distinguished from judgment calls.
	Feedback on boundaries is consistent, with variations in expressions of student performance expected within those boundaries.
Timely	Feedback is delivered incrementally, at precisely the time when students can use it.

In this chapter we have considered the four essential elements of feedback: accuracy, fairness, specificity, and timeliness. For the remainder of the book, we turn our attention to that specific form of feedback known as grades, beginning with an overview of grading issues and the debate that surrounds them.

Chapter 2

THE GRADING
DEBATE

The creation of professional learning communities (DuFour, DuFour, & Eaker, 2008) is perhaps the most pervasive reform in education since 2000. When implemented well, these communities not only learn together but also improve their teaching and leadership decisions in ways that create better opportunities for every student. The very essence of professionalism, however, is the definition of standards for the profession, a process that requires debate that is vigorous, thoughtful, and respectful. Medicine was surely a profession in the 1950s, yet it was also an era in which obstetricians suggested that women who were nervous about pregnancy take up smoking, and psychiatrists defined homosexuality as an illness.

As these two emotionally charged examples suggest, radical changes in professional opinion do not occur easily, but they do occur. Views changed not as a result of sudden enlightenment but as a result of research, debate, and consensus. Physicians disagreed sharply on these issues, but ultimately their commitment to science trumped the prevailing social and political views of the day. Similarly, there are today sharply differing views on grading policies and procedures.

This chapter looks at disagreements over grading policy and the roots of distortions in evaluation and suggests some practical ways to move past them.

Do the Math

The best way to move the grading debate from the theoretical to the practical is by using a single example of improved grading policies. We will employ the highest standard of evidence—mathematical certainty. The essential test of whether you can have a rational discussion about grading is whether the other participants in the debate agree that two plus two equals four. If they say, "Well, that depends on the situation. . . ." then it is unlikely that you can proceed to a logical conclusion. However, if, as I hope is the case, we can separate personal and political beliefs from mathematical certainty, then we can open the door to rational discourse.

Ask your colleagues to complete the following sentence (if you are working alone, then please take a minute or two to complete these lines yourself):

> The differences between a student who earns A's and B's and the student who earns D's and F's are . . .

Common answers to this inquiry include:

- Work ethic
- Parental involvement
- Intelligence
- Homework
- Engagement
- Nutrition
- Attitude
- Test-taking ability
- Prior knowledge
- Organization
- Commitment
- Drug use

In brief, the typical explanations for the differences between the student who earns A's and B's and the student who earns D's and F's center around the characteristics of the students. This is the one thing of which many participants in the grading debate are certain. However, this level of certainty also makes meaningful discussion difficult. If the other participant in a dialogue knows with absolute certainty that the earth is flat and that sailing in a westerly direction from Europe will be a fool's errand, then logic and evidence about the spherical nature of the planet will not be very helpful. You will need a different approach—not logic and evidence, but something that creates personal awareness, such as taking the skeptic up in a balloon at an altitude sufficient to observe with the naked eye the curvature of the earth.

Distortions in Evaluation

How do you shake people with impenetrable certainty out of their convictions? For more than a decade, I have had the opportunity to work with thousands of educators and school administrators around the world. In the course of many presentations, I have been able to challenge their assumptions and, in many cases, influence their professional practices. We begin by establishing what people believe is certain—that the differences between honor students and failing students are accounted for by their personal characteristics. They are diligent or indolent, smart or dumb, solicitous or belligerent. These conclusions about the dichotomy between successful and unsuccessful students are not the exclusive province of excessively judgmental teachers. From athletic competitions to the classroom, we typically assume that the difference between success and failure has to do with the performance of the people we are observing. In fact, however, differences in evaluation can be subject to significant distortions that have nothing to do with performance. Don't believe it? Ask your colleagues to compute the final grade for the student who earned the following marks during a semester:

- C
- C
- MA (missing assignment)
- D
- C
- B

- MA
- MA
- B
- A

Now try it yourself with half a dozen colleagues, asking them to calculate the final grade independently.

Remember, this is the same student, with the same parental involvement, the same intelligence, the same work ethic, the same organization, the same homework, the same nutrition, and so on. For three years, I tracked the responses of more than ten thousand teachers and administrators in audiences throughout the United States, Canada, and Australia. While this is certainly not a random sample and therefore cannot be generalized to all teachers in all countries, the results were nevertheless striking. When they evaluated precisely the same performance by the same student, their final grades were distributed as follows:

- A—7 percent
- B—13 percent
- C—39 percent
- D—21 percent
- F—20 percent

Sometimes I varied the experiment, giving teachers a "mandatory grading policy" such as a 100-point or 4-point scale. Other times I said, "Be as creative as you wish—use any policy that you choose." The results were always the same—whether there was a prescribed grading policy or complete freedom, teachers looked at the same student with the same performance and concluded that the appropriate final grade was F, D, C, B, or A. Even when audiences claimed to have "calibrated" grading systems or "mandatory grading policies" that governed their responses, the variation was consistent. The same student with the same performance might be on the honor roll or might fail, all based upon the idiosyncratic judgment of the teacher or administrator who was assigning the final grade.

If you are a parent and have cross-examined your children about their report cards, you have probably asked them with the incredulity that helps our children mimic their parents so effectively: "How did you get that grade?" Their insouciant response is invariably, "I dunno." The evidence from more than ten thousand teachers suggests that your children are telling you the truth. They *don't* know, because the difference between honor roll grades and failure is not the result of intelligence or work ethic but the result of differences in teacher and administrator judgment.

Moral Imperatives of Grading

Suppose you went to the grocery store and, having selected a pound of potatoes, placed your quarry on a scale, and it read 32 ounces. Perplexed, you placed the same pound of potatoes on another scale, and it read 6 ounces. Not wanting to deceive the merchant, you sought out a third scale, and the same bag of spuds yielded a reading of 14 ounces. You would likely never shop at the store again, because the scales were inconsistent and unreliable.

If a grading system is unfair, then similar performances by different students would be "weighed" differently—in ways that are related not to performance, but to the student's gender or ethnicity, for example. One way to examine the extent to which grading policies are potentially prejudicial is to evaluate the relationship between student performance as measured by grades and the performance of the same students as measured by external indicators. Certainly this method is not perfect—some good students can perform poorly on standardized testing, but when a fundamental skill, such as reading, is at stake, we would expect the relationship to be reasonably strong.

Figure 2.1 (page 36) illustrates a hypothesis that allows for some disconnection between grades and external tests. The bars represent the percentage of students who fail an external reading assessment. The higher bar on the left shows those students who had earned grades of D or F and failed the assessment, and the lower bar on the right shows students who earned grades of A, B, or C, yet still failed the external assessment. As the hypothetical chart suggests, not everybody who earns an A, B, or C is immune from failure on the external test, but it shows that we certainly expect failure to be substantially less likely for those students than for students who earned D's or F's.

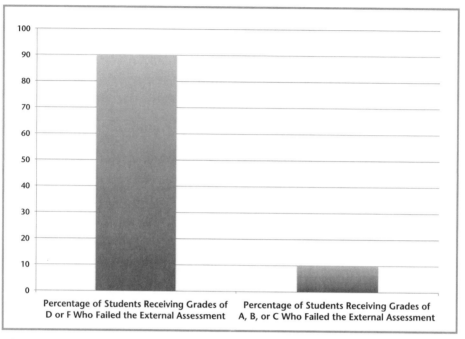

Figure 2.1: Hypothesis—grades are related to performance.

Now consider actual data gathered from more than one thousand ninth- and tenth-grade students. The hypothesis in figure 2.1 is not supported by the evidence, with the number of failures from the D and F students barely higher than the failures by the A, B, and C students, as figure 2.2 illustrates. Since what separated the honor roll students from the failures was not their reading ability, it must be something else.

Is this an isolated example? As figure 2.3 indicates, a similar phenomenon—the disconnection between grades and actual performance—can be observed in different subjects and with very large sample sizes.

Of course, this may not apply to your situation, so consider the following four-step action research project:

1. Generate a hypothesis about the performance of students who fail your state literacy and math exams. What sort of grades do you think they probably receive?

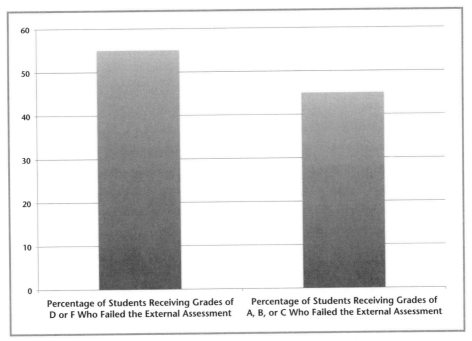

Figure 2.2: Reality—grades are only slightly related to performance.

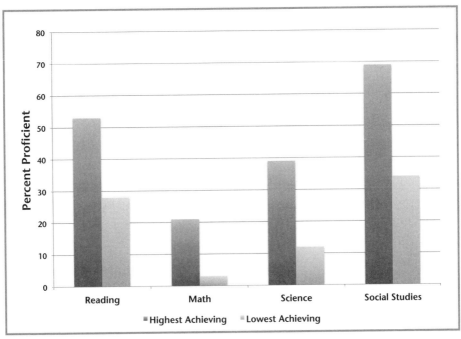

Figure 2.3: Do we tell the truth with letter grades? (Middle school, n > 35,000)

2. Gather a random sample of thirty students who failed your most recent external literacy and math assessments.

3. Look at the actual letter grades of these students. Do you find some passing grades? Do you find some honor roll grades? If so, what does that tell you about the relationship of letter grades in your school to actual student performance?

4. Look at a different sample of students—those who received low grades (D's and F's)—but passed your external literacy and math exams. Can you draw any inferences from these observations?

The point of the exercise is not for me to assert that my research is true for every case. Rather, I would like to suggest that every school should conduct its own inquiry about the relationship between letter grades and student performance.

In order to assess what the "something else" is that separates honor roll from failing students, we will need to conduct some additional inquiry, the kind you could do right now with your students. We will focus on those who earned high grades but failed external examinations. If grades are strictly a reflection of classroom performance, then this subgroup should have the same representation of gender and ethnicity as all the rest of the students. Whether those grades are accurate or erroneous, at least they should be a function of classwork and not gender or ethnicity, right? In the sample from figure 2.2 (page 37), the students were disproportionately minority females. They were perhaps rewarded for being quiet and compliant, but not for being proficient in reading.

Try it for yourself, with just a random sample of thirty students—enough for a rough estimate. Identify students who failed an external exam, and then focus your attention on those who earned A's, B's, and C's. What do you notice? Conversely, examine students who passed an external reading test, but received D's or F's in class. That might suggest students who are proficient, but who are systematically punished for compliance failures. You might want to check to see if that list contains equal numbers of boys and girls and reflects the general ethnic balance of your school.

Standards of Evidence

In order to engage your colleagues effectively in a discussion of grading policy, it will be necessary for each participant to make an honest assessment of his or her claims. Such an honest assessment does not mean that we hold our beliefs with any less conviction, but that we can at the very least distinguish conclusions based upon opinion from those based upon evidence. Before engaging in a debate about grading, consider that the vast majority of participants are likely to have in common a number of beliefs: they want to do what is right for students and for society at large, they want to be successful in their chosen profession, and they want respect from students, parents, colleagues, and society. By identifying common ground, it is more likely that a productive discussion can ensue. The other agreement that is essential at the outset is a consensus on a typology of evidence. Let's review the typology of evidence from the introduction:

1. Opinion

2. Experience

3. Local evidence

4. Preponderance of evidence

5. Mathematical certainty

We have agreed our system of grading must go beyond levels one and two, and we have already considered instances in which the preponderance of evidence is clear: from more than ten thousand teachers, we know that grading policies are strikingly inconsistent. In the final section of this chapter, we will consider an example of how mathematical certainty can be established as the standard to challenge one common grading practice—the use of the zero on a 100-point scale.

Try this experiment with a friend or colleague: Ask, "If we grade students using a 4-point scale, with A = 4, B = 3, C = 2, and D = 1, how many points should we award to a student who fails to turn in any work?" The answer, in almost every case, is zero. Mark the response on figure 2.4 (page 40). (Reproducible forms of figures 2.4, 2.5, and 2.6 may be found on page 126, or visit **go.solution-tree.com/assessment** to download these graphs.)

Figure 2.4: Mark the point value for missing student work.

Now ask, "If we grade students on a 100-point scale, with A = 90, B = 80, C = 70, and D = 60, how many points should we award to a student who fails to turn in any work?" The answer is, surprisingly, still "zero." Mark the response on figure 2.5.

Figure 2.5: Mark the point value for missing student work.

Think about it: in the first case, the difference between the D and failure to turn in any work was 1 point—the same as the interval between A, B, C, and D. But in the second case, the difference between the D and the failure to turn in any work was 60 points. Because we changed from a 4-point scale to a 100-point scale, we suddenly believed that the failure of a student to turn in assigned work was six times worse than doing the work wretchedly—the quality that most accurately described D-level work.

Now, return to the original question about the 4-point scale, where A = 4, B = 3, C = 2, and D = 1. Ask the question again, "How many points are awarded for the student who fails to hand in work?" The answer, again, will be "zero." However, if we are logically consistent, our response would have to be "minus six"—that is, the penalty for failing to hand in work would be six times greater than D-level work. In my work with tens of thousands of teachers and administrators, I have never seen a single instance of someone suggesting that minus six is the correct score for a student. Consider figure 2.6 in the light of responses to figures 2.4 and 2.5, and then ask your friends and colleagues who were so certain just a few moments earlier why the zero on a 100-point scale makes sense.

Figure 2.6: Mark the point value for missing student work.

It is not a matter of opinion that the zero on a 100-point scale is wrong—it's a matter of mathematics. No participant in the discussion has ever considered the grade of minus six for missing work—that would be bizarre, irrational, and wrong. However, many educators commit this very mistake when they use the zero on a 100-point scale. This is a head-snapping moment for some, but not all, people who consider the issue. There are many commonly used justifications for the use of the zero:

- "If students turn in zero work, then they deserve a zero. It's obvious!"

- "If failure to turn in work is the same interval as the other grades, then we would have to give students a 50—10 points below a D—for doing nothing. That's giving points away for doing nothing."

- "Of course it's a harsh punishment—if we don't do that, then students would never turn in their work."

- "If we don't use zeroes, it's not fair to the students who do turn their work in on time."

While each of these statements will be offered with conviction, let's use the typology of evidence to evaluate them:

- What students "deserve" is a moral judgment.

- The "50 points for doing nothing" argument is a straw man, an argument introduced solely for the sake of ridiculing it. There are, as we shall see in future chapters, many better consequences for missing work than either the zero or the fifty.

- The claim that punishment is an effective inducement for students to submit work is a testable hypothesis and does not require extensive experimentation. All we need to do is examine levels of homework compliance with teachers who have used the zero on a 100-point scale for many years and inquire whether the level of homework compliance is higher today than it was several years ago. If their hypothesis is correct, then word of their punishment policies will have spread among students, and, fearful of the zero, students in each successive year should be more compliant.

- The claim that failure to use an inaccurate and ineffective grading policy for some students would be unfair to others is illogical. By the same reasoning, failure to use corporal punishment on misbehaving students could be construed as unfair to students who behave, though few educators today would endorse corporal punishment. Second, it misses a profoundly greater issue of unfairness, which is the varying effects that grading policies have on students from different socioeconomic backgrounds, family structures, and home environments. Some students go home to attentive parents who make homework a priority, while others go home to parents who are busy, absent, preoccupied, or indifferent. Others go home to chaos. To assume that the first group of students is good and deserves rewards while the other two groups deserve punishment is profoundly unfair.

This chapter has suggested that the most well-intentioned grading systems can lead to inaccuracy, unfairness, and lack of specificity. In the next chapter, we will look at ways to improve the first of the four crucial elements of any grading system, accuracy.

Chapter 3

HOW TO IMPROVE
ACCURACY

In the previous chapter, we looked at the grading debate and considered how inaccuracies affect grading systems. While no grading system is perfect, we can take clear and definitive steps toward improving the processes and practices of grading.

Sometimes teachers defend the accuracy of a grade because the final result conforms to the mathematical system that they have created, but this sort of numerical precision creates only the illusion of accuracy. For example, the use of the arithmetic mean, or average, might be calculated accurately, but however accurate it might be, the use of the average undermines accuracy in grading. You would never, for example, decide whether or not to wear a coat on January 31 based on the average temperature during the month. You would want to know the temperature on that day and make your decision accordingly.

In this chapter, we'll first explore how to measure accuracy, and then we will look at how to improve it.

Measuring Accuracy

Let's continue the analogy to temperature. Jacqueline B. Clymer and Dylan Wiliam (2006/2007) suggest that we think about the relationship between grades and temperature this way: a thermostat provides information about the current temperature, just as a grade should tell us what a student knows and can do at the moment. A thermostat also gives us a way to set the temperature we would like to have, just as a feedback-oriented grading system shows clearly a standard that students must achieve. This information reveals the difference between where students are now and where they need to be, just as we know that raising the room temperature from fifty to seventy degrees will require more energy than if we were seeking to raise the temperature only two degrees. Finally, as in a heating system, where we have a choice of interventions—heat, cold, fan, or nothing—a teacher can decide which strategies to use based on the feedback she is receiving (Clymer & Wiliam, 2006/2007).

An eighth-grade science teacher transformed this theory into action by creating a system with these features:

- Assessments were designed to provide feedback—they were not the final grade.

- Grade records were informative, allowing both the student and teacher to understand that different starting points are required for different students.

- Feedback was continuous and flexible. Grades could rise or fall based upon student performance.

- Final grades were based on the student's actual work and achievement, not the intelligence, aptitude, and prior knowledge that the student had before the class had begun.

Student response to this system was overwhelmingly positive. Not only did the vast majority of students understand the fundamental principle of this system—that their personal effort and continuous learning were the primary causes of their grade—they also appreciated the fact that their grades could always be improved. These middle school students asked more questions, became more involved in their learning, and liked the specific and detailed feedback.

Some critics assail case studies and other action research because they lack the elegance of a true experiment, with random assignment of students to control and experimental groups (Campbell & Stanley, 1963). While formal research is important, we should not neglect the value of action-research observations such as that shared by Clymer and Wiliam (2006/2007). In fact, Clymer was able to control experiments far better than many people who did more formal projects.

Think about it: it was the same teacher, with the same curriculum, same school, and the same or very similar student characteristics before and after her grading experiment. The only major change was the new grading system. Therefore, we can be reasonably confident that it was that change—a consistent, accurate, feedback-oriented grading system—that led to improvements in student performance and engagement.

Thus, we can claim that grades are accurate only when those grades reflect what students know and can do when the grade is awarded. This means that the use of the average is almost always inaccurate, unless student performance oscillates around the mean throughout the year. For the average to accurately represent student performance, student "progress" would look something like figure 3.1, an unlikely and disappointing experience.

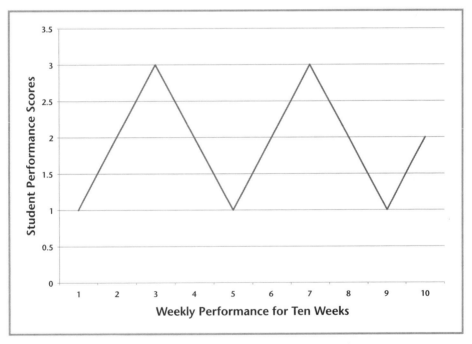

Figure 3.1: The rare instance in which the average score is accurate.

This unfortunate student made progress at first, but then dropped back to where he started. Most teachers observing this would intervene, recognizing that something was wrong with the student's performance and engagement, and that perhaps improvements were needed in teaching and feedback. The virtue of this example is that it illustrates the very rare instance in which the arithmetic mean, or average, meets our standard of accuracy, since the grade represents student performance at the end of the marking period. Of course, most student performance is not at all like that depicted in the figure. Student performance is not stagnant; it improves over time. Figure 3.2 is far more representative of real student performance, in which students begin slowly, receive feedback, become more motivated and competent, receive more feedback, and ultimately demonstrate gains.

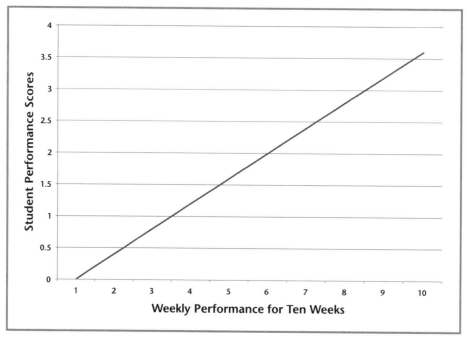

Figure 3.2: Steady progress, the more typical student performance.

Compare the student performances in figures 3.1 (page 45) and 3.2. Would you agree that they are significantly different? The first student made fits and starts, but never sustained any gains in learning. The student represented in figure 3.2 made steady progress, ending the year at 3.6, a significant improvement—but *this student's average is the same as that of the student in figure 3.1.* It would not be accurate to say that both should receive the same grade; grading systems that use the average—even when they carry out the calculation of the average with great mathematical precision to several decimal places—are wrong. The real life of the classroom is not linear, and it involves fits and starts, success and failure. Some lessons result in "aha!" moments, and some leave students bewildered. It still happens to me every week. Almost always, however, by the end of the term, we have made significant progress.

A more accurate description of classroom life is represented in figure 3.3.

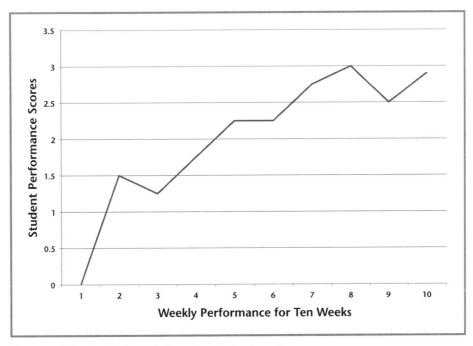

Figure 3.3: Realistic variations in student performance.

These sorts of variations are common, with some weeks punctuated by gains and others by losses; occasionally the performance is level. Sometimes these variations are due to teacher actions, and other times there is social drama, distraction or encouragement at home, support from peers, technology disasters, or any number of other week-to-week vicissitudes that prevent student performance from achieving the artificial linearity of figure 3.2. However messy the reality of figure 3.3, that student's performance deserves a higher grade than the student performance represented in figure 3.1 (page 45).

In sum, the use of the average may appear to be precise, but it is not accurate, because it does not meet our standard of accurately reflecting student performance.

How can you assess the accuracy of your grades? Start by working backward—identify students who, at the end of the year, have the same letter grade. I find that this is most effective when you consider students with the grade of B, because it is commonly one of the least-accurate grades if the standard of accuracy is a reflection of student performance. Once you have assembled a small sample of students with the same final grade, look at their performance. How is it similar? How is it different?

Consider three vignettes of student performance in a secondary school math class. Each of these students received a final grade of B. While the descriptions and names are fictional composites of many students, the reader can judge the extent to which these examples ring true.

Sean

Sean received a B because of his exceptional effort and diligence. He turned in homework every day (though the answers were seldom correct). Each time he received a D or F on a quiz, he would come to class and ask for help, and the teacher would work through the problems with him. Sean also completed an extra credit project that was very creative, creating a mural with mathematical equations in a caption over one of the people he depicted. Finally, he received "citizenship points" for his good behavior during class.

Sam

Sam received a B, because his surly attitude and rude and disrespectful behavior deserved, in the teacher's opinion, some sort of consequence. It seemed as if his papers, always accurate and submitted on time, had been wadded up deliberately. Sam would finish every quiz and test before the rest of the class, and he would smirk at his fellow students who were still laboring to complete their work. But the final straw was when Sam cut several classes. He thought that because he had submitted his homework in advance (flawless, as usual), and there were no quizzes or tests on those days, he could get away with it. But the departmental policy is clear—unexcused absences result in a zero for the day, and that brought his A+ performance to a B grade. Another colleague who had observed the entire affair concurred, saying, "The jerk got what he deserved."

Maryellen

Maryellen was an average student. She did most of her homework, received C's and B's on her quizzes, and with some extra credit, was able to get a C+ on the final exam. She never gave the teacher any trouble, and her parents were strong and vocal supporters of the school. With a little extra credit, Mary, too, received a final grade of B.

When the same grade is associated with wildly different levels of performance, the grading system is inaccurate. The same technique—working backward from a grade to examine the relationship between the grade and student performance—can also be used with individual pieces of student work. In an experiment with fifty classroom educators, I provided an example of student work that had been awarded a B and then removed the grade and any identifying information that would reveal the name of the student, teacher, or school involved. I then asked these teachers to assign their own grade to the work. In twelve different work samples, I found that the grades from other teachers varied widely. Guskey and Bailey (2001) came to similar findings, noting that it did not matter whether the grading system was subjective—as, for example, in grades associated with student writing—or objective, such as grades that are commonly associated with mathematics. *All* the grades were subjective, because the same performance resulted in different grades.

Practical Strategies to Improve Accuracy

Although every endeavor involving human judgment is subject to error, we can nevertheless make efforts to identify, quantify, and reduce it. For teachers, this is a continuous process, and we never achieve an error-free state of perfection. We can, however, make significant improvements in the accuracy of grading through the frequent use of reality checks, collaborative scoring, and the avoidance of unintentional mathematical distortions in our grading policies.

Reality Checks

The two essential reality checks for grading are the comparison of student results to external measurements and the determination of whether students are receiving behavioral grades.

External Measurements

For some courses, the learning objectives of the class are closely aligned to external assessments. Examples of this close alignment would be courses that are associated with Advanced Placement (AP), International Baccalaureate (IB), Cambridge International Examinations (CIE), or other standard assessments that are directly linked to a class curriculum. In these cases, a high score in the class should be strongly associated with high scores on the external exams. When there is a divergence, then there are only a few possible explanations. If the external exam results are lower than the classroom scores, we might conclude that the student just had a bad day or that the items on the test were unusually difficult.

However, if this happens with more than a few students, two other explanations are more likely. First, the taught curriculum and the tested curriculum are not aligned. This is particularly likely to happen when teachers are unfamiliar with the external examination or if they retain a strong affinity for their previously used curriculum. In these cases, the tested curriculum is treated as an extra burden rather than the academic core of the course. By contrast, teachers who are deeply familiar with the external examination—particularly those teachers who have served as official examiners for the testing organization and read hundreds of examinations from students in other schools—have an exceptional advantage. They not only know their subjects, but they also know how students will be evaluated. The closer the relationship between classroom teaching and external assessment, the lower the chance for error caused by misalignment.

Behavioral Grades

The second and more common cause of divergence between grades and external results is the conflation of academic performance and behavior. When grades are high and external results are low, we should ask how much of the academic grade is, in fact, a behavioral grade. Girls in particular are rewarded for quiet and compliant behavior, and the result is that they are strikingly overrepresented on honor rolls and in membership in the National Honor Society. Girls also matriculate in college in significantly higher numbers than boys (Kafer, 2005). However, when it comes to performance on external examinations, the gender gap ranges from narrow to inconsistent to sometimes absent (Reeves, 2006a). While girls have learned to please teachers, they have not necessarily achieved at higher academic levels. Conversely, when grades are low and external results are high, we should consider the possibility that the low grades were a reflection of behavior that displeased the teacher. In both cases, these are grave inaccuracies in grading. The error is not in the attempt by teachers to encourage good behavior. The error is the mislabeling of behavior as "algebra" or "chemistry" or "history." If we wish to address student behavior in an effective manner, then let us call it what it is.

Of course, for most teachers, there is no convenient external exam, such as Advanced Placement or Cambridge International Examinations, to serve as a reality check for a comparison of classroom grades and academic success. However, many other sources of information can help focus grades on academic performance and reduce the probability of inaccuracy. The use of academic performance scoring rubrics, for example, allows teachers to focus exclusively on the knowledge and skills of a student. Our rubrics might make reference, for example, to the design of experiments that test a hypothesis, rather than state that "the student will test hypotheses with a cheerful and compliant disposition."

Collaborative Scoring

Perhaps one of the best and most practical ways to improve accuracy is the collaborative scoring of student work. This is also a superb professional learning experience, allowing teachers to improve the quality, consistency, and timeliness of their feedback to students. Sometimes collaborative scoring occurs informally, as when a teacher asks a colleague for help: "I'm on the fence about this particular project—how would you evaluate it?"

However, the most effective collaborative scoring processes I have observed follow a consistent protocol in which the identities of the students and teachers are unknown to the teachers who are doing the scoring. The only question is, "Given this particular piece of student work and the scoring rubric I have available, what is my assessment of the work?" Accuracy improves not only because practice with a rubric leads to consistency, but also because teachers have constructive discussions about their disagreements. This leads to an improvement in the clarity and specificity of the scoring rubric. Figure 3.4 illustrates improvements over time with the same teachers engaging in collaborative scoring of student work. The vertical axis represents the percentage of agreement among teachers, and the bars represent the first, second, third, and fourth practice sessions.

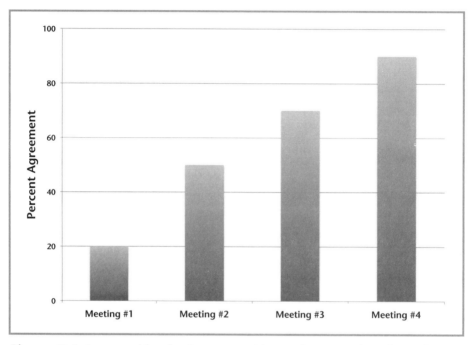

Figure 3.4: Improved levels of agreement in grading over time through collaboration.

Finally, the use of collaborative scoring techniques gives students feedback that is timelier. This is because teachers use scoring rubrics more frequently, and as they refine the clarity and specificity of these rubrics, they are able to evaluate complex assessments more quickly. Figure 3.5 demonstrates the impact of consistent practice on the speed of grading. The vertical axis represents the minutes required to score an assignment, and the bars represent once again the first, second, third, and fourth practice sessions. With practice, accuracy improved and so did timeliness. Ask yourself when you last had a professional learning experience that both improved the quality of instruction in a key area—feedback—and also saved time for teachers?

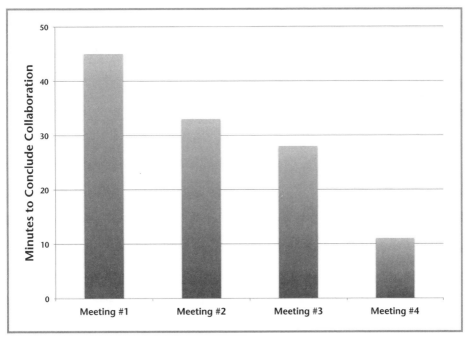

Figure 3.5: Improved speed of collaborative grading over time.

Avoiding Mathematical Distortions

The last practical method of improving accuracy has to do with the avoidance of inadvertent mathematical errors. Earlier, we addressed how the zero on a 100-point scale creates mathematical distortion. Some schools use the "50 minimum" policy to avoid this distortion.

Unfortunately, this leads to a good deal of political discontent, because it appears to critics that students are being given 50 points without doing any work. Therefore, if it is psychologically necessary for stakeholders in your area to have the zero as an option for teachers, then we can remove its mathematically distorting impact by using a 4-point scale rather than a 100-point scale. This may require some adjustments to computerized grading systems, but it is not impossible. If teachers wish to preserve the fine distinctions among students that the 100-point system creates, so that they can distinguish between the bragging rights of students with an 85.6 instead of an 84.3, then the same precision can be used with the 4-point scale by allowing several places to the right of the decimal point. However, then when a zero is used, it cannot, by definition, have an impact any greater than 1 point below the D, which is worth 1 point.

The other source of mathematical distortion, as we learned at the beginning of this chapter, is the average, or arithmetic mean. The best alternatives to the average are the use of accumulating points, or the ability of the teacher to weight end-of-year assignments much higher than early assignments, in the same way that track coaches consider times at the end of the season more relevant than those at the beginning. Similarly, when students are creating computer programs, their work is not judged on the average number of errors in the program during the semester but on the quality of their program at the end of the year. The same is true in art and music—and there is no reason that this sort of thoughtful judgment cannot be applied in every academic subject. Computerized grading systems that default to the average are simply wrong, and teachers must have the ability to override their mindless calculations in order to substitute a superior grading policy that links student grades to student performance *when the grade is awarded*, rather than at the end of the year.

No matter how accurate grades are, however, they will not be credible with stakeholders if they are not fair. In the next chapter, we consider the second element of grading—fairness.

Chapter 4

HOW TO IMPROVE FAIRNESS

One of the most disturbing trends in grades is the predominance of females over males on middle and high school honor rolls. This leads, in turn, to a significant advantage in females over males in college enrollment (Kafer, 2005). If the data suggested that women were significantly more intelligent than men (an argument some readers may be willing to make), then there would be nothing wrong with the apparent female advantage in educational performance. However, if we stipulate that—for the sake of argument—women are only somewhat smarter than men, something is clearly wrong with a grading system that inflates scores based on gender. In this chapter, we will consider the extent to which grading is not merely a reflection of student performance, but can sometimes be inappropriately influenced by the student's gender, ethnicity, and socioeconomic status.

Almost everyone wants to be fair, and most of us think that we are fair, particularly when it comes to making decisions about children. The fact that some students do better than others is part of life. There are winners and losers in athletics, mathematics, writing, music, and many other endeavors. The work of K. Anders Ericcson, Neil Charness, Robert Hoffman, and Paul Feltovich (2006), as well as that of Hattie (2009), suggests strongly that deliberate practice is what separates top performers from others. Stanford researcher Carol Dweck (2006) admonishes parents to praise children for their work ethic, not their innate ability, so that young people will learn to adopt a mindset that associates growth with hard work. In school, we have honor rolls, valedictorians, and scholarships to honor the efforts of those who work harder than others, or so the theory goes. This chapter explores the hypothesis that academic rewards and punishments are, in fact, bestowed fairly.

What Does Fairness Really Mean?

Fairness is not a philosophically elusive concept. Many readers of this chapter have, at some point in their lives, been on a school playground and heard the plaintive wail, "That's not fair!" Perhaps a child received assistance from another student in what should have been an individual performance, stepped outside the boundaries of the game, or otherwise flouted the rules that almost all young children engaged in playground activities can understand and apply. Kids don't mind losing—not nearly as much as their parents do—but they are offended by cheating. On the playground, when students perceive that a game is unfair, they simply stop playing. Fairness is not just about the existence of rules and their careful enforcement.

As we move from the playground to the classroom, fairness means that the evaluation of a student is based on the performance of that student. On the soccer field, it would be unfair (though not out of the realm of possibility) for a parent to leap in front of the goal to prevent an opponent from scoring. What about when a parent helps a child on homework, writes a fabricated excuse for missing work, or appeals to the administration for reconsideration of a low grade? If we accept that fairness means the evaluation of a student is based on that student's performance, then we must also be clear that the evaluation of a student is *not* a function of any of the following:

- Work claimed by the student that, in fact, was performed by others

- Tools available to one student but not available to other students

- Influence available to one student but not available to other students

The formulation seems reasonable enough, until we consider the real world of the classroom, in which different levels of assistance, tools, and influence are not only common but intentional. Some of these differences are not the result of parents who are preoccupied with the success of their own children. Students with disabilities, for example, receive assistance that is not available to other students; this includes special education teachers, assistive technology, and teams of advocates. Moreover, great teachers routinely make themselves available to provide additional help to struggling students, and outstanding schools create intervention programs for students who need personal and intentional support to succeed.

Suddenly, the concept of fairness becomes much more problematic. Evaluation is not, it turns out, merely a function of the performance of a single student, because that formulation of fairness depends upon an assumption that is deeply flawed—the assumption that all students enter the classroom with equal advantages, equal access to support, and equal backgrounds. Educational systems do not provide an environment of fairness when they merely confirm the disparities with which students begin their schooling. The challenge is how to reconcile the need for different levels of support for students with the need to provide grading and feedback that are accurate and fair.

Some schools have attempted to address this challenge by noting on report cards that a grade or evaluation mark was achieved "with assistance." This may be a useful indicator, provided it is used on a consistent and rational basis. If, however, the "with assistance" notation is used only for special education students who received the assistance of a special education teacher, but not for privileged students who surreptitiously received the assistance of parents and tutors, then we have hardly reached any reasonable standard of fairness.

In sum, when we say a grade is "fair," what we really mean is that the grade is a reflection of the student's performance and the context of that performance. That is why a lone letter or number can rarely provide a fair representation. The same grade of B- could mean:

- Outstanding effort and perseverance, but the student has not yet met grade-level standards
- Outstanding performance well above grade level, but the student's attitude, work ethic, and class participation are inadequate

- Superior performance, except for one incident of cheating that resulted in a score of zero on a major exam

- Failure to meet all academic standards, but the student earned several "extra credit" points to merit the final grade

If you are the college admissions officer looking at a transcript, the parent examining a report card, or the teacher of a new class attempting to learn more about your students, you will see none of these explanations, only the grade of B-. The grade without context is without much meaning. Fairness, it turns out, is a quality that has implications not only for the student earning the grade but also for other people who use the information represented by that grade.

Why Does Fairness Matter?

When we consider the issue of fairness in school, there is a significant consequence to our efforts. When we succeed at fairness, more students are engaged in the pursuit of academic excellence, and parents, future teachers, colleges, and other stakeholders trust us. When we fail, students withdraw, and we produce cynicism and distrust. The widespread belief that grades are not fair leads, unfortunately, to a greater reliance on simple mathematical formulas that depend solely upon standardized tests (Lehrer, 2009). Moreover, when perceptions of unfairness are pervasive, there is a hidden impact on student motivation. Girls are not underrepresented in math and science disciplines because of neurological differences, but because they have received the relentless message, from early adolescence to graduate school, that these disciplines are part of a man's world. When there are enormous imbalances in student success based on gender, the society at large has suffered, because half the available brainpower did not attempt to play the game.

The point is not just that we should have more women in math and science but that, as a society, we benefit when we have more *people* in math and science—and in teaching, art criticism, psychiatry, culinary art, neurosurgery, or any other field. If we wish to cultivate excellence at the top of any field, then we need more people who are willing to engage in the attempt. Failures at fairness limit not only opportunities for the individual student, but the size of the pool of potentially outstanding performers in every discipline.

Equity in Grading Self-Assessment

The reproducible Equity in Grading Self-Assessment (pages 127–130 and online at **go.solution-tree.com/assessment**) provides a nonjudgmental guide for teachers and educational administrators who are willing to explore the extent to which their grading systems, and the applications of those systems, are fair and equitable. This self-assessment is designed for classroom use, but it can be modified for use by an entire school or school system.

Certainly, it is possible that this exercise will reveal nothing of significance and that, in fact, it will confirm a high degree of equity in your grading system, but it is also possible that you will make observations that are comparable to the following, which I have seen when I have worked through these data with teachers:

- Students with honor-roll grades but low scores on external tests are more likely to be female, and in urban systems they tend to be minority female students. This observation is consistent with national data that suggest that female students perform markedly better than males in high school and matriculate in college by a significantly higher percentage compared to their male classmates (Kafer, 2005). Girls are also significantly overrepresented in academic recognitions that are exclusively reflective of grades.

- Students with low grades and good scores are more likely to be male, and in urban systems, they tend to be minority males. Rebelliousness and defiance among adolescent boys are hardly a news flash, and in the power struggles of middle and high schools, one of the few tools available to teachers is the grading system. Boys accumulate F's and zeroes even as their analytical ability improves. In fact, punitive grading systems serve as a reward, telling them that "no make-up" rules mean more free time.

The foregoing points may strike you, as they have other readers, as offensive overgeneralizations, but before you come to that conclusion, please do the following experiment for your school, as I was compelled to do with mine:

- How many girls were inducted into the National Honor Society last year? How many boys? What is the ratio, and how does that compare to your student population?
- What was the ratio of girls to boys on the honor roll?
- What was the ratio of girls to boys who failed classes?
- What is the gender ratio in remedial courses? In advanced courses?

See for yourself if a clear pattern emerges in your school. These observations are not merely a lament for under-rewarded boys, but also a genuine concern for over-rewarded girls. In qualitative observations I have conducted in urban systems about girls on the honor roll who failed to pass basic literacy and math tests, I heard a disturbing consistency to comments on the performance of these young women:

- "She never gives me any trouble."
- "She's very quiet."
- "She attends class almost every day."
- "She always turns in her homework."

These comments, however well-intended, reflect a focus on compliant behavior rather than academic proficiency.

Social Class and Grading

One of the most important predictors of success in high school and college is the extent to which students learn to "play school"— that is, they know when to ask for help, who can be reliable sources of assistance, and how to fit in with the prevailing expectations of authority figures. Orlando Griego (educator and founder of the La Familia project) was formerly head of a postsecondary institution in Colorado with the largest ethnic minority population in the western United States. Griego noticed (personal communication, January 3,

1994), that while young Latinas were enrolling in college in record numbers, they were also failing many classes, particularly in math and science. The numbers were particularly alarming for students who had children. The family, not school, was the center of their lives. Their sense of family obligation was different from that of students who were young and unmarried. Even for Latina students who were young and single, the responsibility for childcare, he found, frequently extended to nieces, nephews, younger siblings, and other members of the extended family. Their roles as caregivers were an important part of their identity, and academic success depended upon integrating academics within this social structure and not making alienation of the family the price for achievement.

Griego created the La Familia project in order to build a family-oriented supportive environment for Latina students. The students were given their own room for study, food, socializing, and academic support. They were able to find assignments and test dates online and didn't need to explain to the professor why they missed a class to care for a sick child. They were able to learn the fundamentals that their course syllabi had assumed they had already mastered. They were also recognized publicly as "La Familia Scholars," a term that included the precise blend of their pursuits but also signaled to the family and academic communities the priority that family and scholarship played in their lives. Griego's efforts paid off, reducing dramatically the Latina drop-out rate. More importantly, he provided a model for the entire college system of how a commitment to equity need not compromise academic rigor but does need to take into account the needs of a diverse student body.

Accuracy and fairness are essential elements of grading, but they are not sufficient to form a fully satisfactory system of student evaluation. Grading systems must also be effective, a complex requirement that includes specific and timely feedback on student achievement. In the next chapter, we will explore how teachers and school leaders can establish more specific grading systems.

Chapter 5

HOW TO IMPROVE
SPECIFICITY

Although specificity is a key to improved grading practices, most grading systems engage in the strange practice of reducing a complex set of variables into a single letter or number. Grading should be designed to improve communication, making clear to students, fellow teachers, and future teachers the academic performance of a student. Effective communication is impossible, however, if the people involved do not know or agree on what the relationship is between performance and the numeric or letter symbols that appear in grades. If you received feedback on your performance written in ancient Egyptian hieroglyphs, then no matter how well-intentioned the teacher who provided the feedback, it is unlikely you would learn much from the exchange. It is not that the work and thought put into the grading system are not impressive—many teachers invest a lot of time and work in their grading systems. Unfortunately, these documents seek to provide a rationale that makes sense to the designer and administrator of the system, but are sometimes utterly without communicative value to students, parents, fellow teachers, and other school systems that may want to evaluate the transcript in the future.

One of the principal controversies in grading is the extent to which grading should be limited to the demonstration of academic ability by students and the degree to which it should reflect a range of other characteristics, including work habits and personal character. Ken O'Connor (2009, p. 250) is a leading advocate of the principle that "effort, participation, attitude, and other behaviors shall not be included in grades." Critics often respond, "But don't you *care* about attendance, attitude, and behavior? In the real world, our graduates will be evaluated based upon these matters every day!" A careful reading of O'Connor reveals that he cares very much about these matters. He cares so much about "effort, participation, attitude, and behavior" that he suggests that teachers should label these variables "effort, participation, attitude, and behavior" and not "math, English, history, and science." It is precisely because these and other characteristics are important that we should improve the specificity of grading.

Gauging Knowledge

The best way to grade what a student is able to know and do is to report specific student performance relative to an objective standard. Many kindergarten report cards do this with clarity and precision, specifying, for example, the numbers and letters a student knows. Physical fitness and music tests also tend toward this degree of clarity, communicating the number of exercises that a student can perform or the key signatures of the scales and arpeggios that a young musician can play. We can, if we choose, do the same in other subjects, using tools such as the standards achievement report, an example of which appears in figure 5.1.

Note well that teachers need not use the standards achievement report *in place of* a traditional letter grade. Secondary schools in particular feel compelled to use letter grades to produce a transcript, and there are cultural imperatives in many educational systems that make the designation of a letter grade essential. Therefore, the argument in favor of improving specificity is not about eliminating letter grades; it is a suggestion to communicate about them in a manner that is clearer and more meaningful for students, parents, and fellow teachers.

Translating Standards Into Grades

How do we translate standards achievement into grades? One simple system considers a combination of student performance and ultimate performance during a term. Suppose there are six assessments during a term. An assessment could be a research paper, an in-class test, a lab, a demonstration, or other significant evidence of

Washington High School
Standards Achievement Report 2001–2002

Student Name: _____

Class: _Biology_ _____ **Teacher:** _____

E = Exemplary; **P** = Proficient; **IP** = In Progress; **N** = Not Meeting Standard

Assignment	Standard						
	1 Biodiversity	2 Genetics	3 Cell Structure	4 Environmental Interrelationships	5 Explanation of Scientific Conclusions	6 Teamwork	7 Submission of Work on Time
Lab 1	P			P	P	E	N
Analytical paper 1	P				P		IP
Lab 2	P				P	E	IP
Analytical paper 2		P			P		IP
Lab 3			E		E	E	N
Analytical paper 3			E		E		IP
Synthesis 1	P	E	E		E		IP
Lab 4				P	P	E	IP
Analytical paper 4				P		P	IP
Lab 5		P		P	P	E	N
Analytical paper 5		E		E	E		IP
Lab 6				P	E	E	P
Analytical paper 6				E	E	E	P
Synthesis 2	E	E	E	P	E		P

Figure 5.1: Sample standards achievement report.

Note: Not every assignment encompasses every standard, but every assignment addresses several of the most important standards for this class. Moreover, the teacher has clearly identified that there are both academic and behavioral standards for students. This particular report is the profile of a student who is "proficient" or "exemplary" in every academic standard, but who displays a rather consistent inability to turn work in on time. The feedback that is provided by this report is far more revealing than the letter grade.

student learning. In this example, we will assume that each assessment is evaluated on a 4-point scale:

4 = Exemplary

3 = Proficient

2 = Progressing, but not yet proficient—more work is required

1 = Not meeting standards—the student requires intensive intervention and extensive work in order to make progress

As these labels suggest, the numbers 4, 3, 2, and 1 do not nearly translate into letter grades of A, B, C, and D, because a grade of C typically qualifies a student for work at the next level. In this standards-based system, however, a score of 2 is not proficient work. The labels also imply that the evaluations of each assessment are not designed as a final determination of student ability but rather as feedback to improve learning. The score of 2 does not mean "You didn't do very well, but move on to the next assignment anyway." Rather, scores of 1 and 2 explicitly require additional work. Nevertheless, there comes a time when grades are due, so how can teachers communicate both a clear record of student progress and a letter grade? Here is one system to consider:

A = At least four assessments with a final score of 4 and two assessments with a final score of at least 3

B = At least four assessments with a final score of at least 3 and two assessments with a final score of at least 2

C = At least three assessments with a final score of at least 3

Feedback and Improvement

Let us stop and consider the important implications of this system so far. First, the use of the term *final score* suggests that students submit their work, get feedback, and improve. The A student, therefore, is not necessarily the one who received a score of 4 upon the first submission of every assignment but rather the student who respected the teacher's feedback, worked harder, and ultimately received the better evaluation. This strategy encourages work ethic, respect, and determination. Dweck (2006) and A. L. Duckworth, Christopher Peterson,

Michael Matthews, and Dennis Kelly (2007) have contributed land-mark research to the field, indicating that these characteristics—what Duckworth calls "grit"—are among the most important not only for student success but for later academic and work success.

Quality, Not Just Quantity

A second implication of this system is that teachers are emphasizing quality rather than quantity in work. While the grade of C typically is associated with work of poor quality, in this system the grade of C required that students submit—and most probably resubmit—work that meets the standards of proficiency established for the class. However, the C students completed only three of the assessments at this level of quality. These students were not rewarded for a large quantity of work that was of low quality, since they were being asked to focus on meeting the requirements for proficiency. In other words, submitting three pieces of work three times—a total of nine submissions—leads to a higher level of quality and greater respect for teacher feedback than is the case when the same student submits nine pieces of work one time but never uses teacher feedback to improve performance.

Avoiding "the Coward's F"

A third implication of this system is that there is no D, a grade I have described as "the coward's F." When the possibility of a D is part of a grading system, it legitimizes the worst of all possible worlds, in which students can pass a class and proceed to the next level of instruction with the virtually certain prospect of failure. Worse yet, the availability of a D encourages the least-motivated student to do the least possible amount of work. While some teachers use the D as a punishment for poor work and inadequate motivation, the D is, in fact, a reward for bad behavior. It tells the student, "You really don't have to listen to the teacher, resubmit the assignment, or redo the work. Just do enough papers, quickly and badly, and we'll let you skate through to the next grade."

Listening to Students

In order to determine whether these conclusions are appropriate for students in your school, you might consider doing what I did—ask the students. It will be important to do so in an environment that is confidential and anonymous. Therefore, the faculties of two schools might want to agree to a reciprocal action research project, in which the teacher-researchers of Washington School interview the students at Jefferson School, and vice versa. I have been fortunate enough to conduct personal interviews and focus groups with many students on this subject, asking them about which grading systems lead to higher levels of achievement. Body piercings have, at least so far, not penetrated the frontal lobes of these students, because they respond to my questions with astonishing insight. One secondary school student, whose anonymity I guaranteed, said this regarding the grading system above: "I hate it. Last year you could do anything and get a D, but now you have to work really hard to get even a C. In fact, it's such a hassle to get a C, you might as well get a B."

Although several other students echoed this sentiment, I am acutely aware of the limits of interviews and focus groups, non-random samples that cannot be generalized to a larger population. When I interviewed more than ninety teachers and parents on the same subject, the responses were stunningly similar. When students are required to submit work, they are not happy about it, but they nevertheless perform at a higher level. This conclusion is, for many teachers—particularly those whose job security is sometimes related to their degree of popularity with students and parents—a difficult dilemma. "To what extent can I risk making students mad?" they wonder. "What if I am effective as a teacher, but unpopular with my students?" Fortunately, the landmark work of Australian researcher Herbert Marsh (1984) has resolved this dilemma. Marsh is the creator of the SEEQ—Student Evaluation of Educational Quality—and a prolific researcher and writer. With more than one million administrations, the reliability and validity of his student survey instrument have been established independently. In sum, Marsh documents what most parents and teachers—particularly parents and teachers of adolescents—know to be true: students crave challenges. While they rarely appreciate it in the moment, they admire most teachers who demand their best. Conversely, students disdain patronization, ridiculing teachers who think that the way to the students' hearts and minds is through low expectations.

What About the Real World?

My extensive correspondence, received both personally and vicariously through the blogosphere, suggests that many defenders of traditional grading systems believe the "real world" does not allow multiple opportunities for success. "You know it or you don't" is a common refrain, as is "In the real world, you've got to get it right the first time." This is a hypothesis that can be tested at once. Select some people you respect—physicians, scientists, electricians, pilots, architects, engineers, attorneys who practice before the Supreme Court, diplomats, plumbers, teachers, mechanics—and then pose this question: "Is the model of professional success that has served you best one that insists upon a one-shot performance with success upon the first attempt, or is your model of success 'Try it, get feedback, then improve it; try it again, get feedback, then improve it again'?"

The stakes could not be higher, whether it is the engineer and architect who design the skyscraper or the electrician who must depend upon his or her calculations while balanced precariously in the air. The appellate attorney in a capital case bears a heavy responsibility, as does the teacher who will either nurture the ability of your child to read or alienate that child from learning. What do the best of the best in these professions really do in the real world? As a rash of new research suggests (Colvin, 2008; Ericcson et al., 2006; Gladwell, 2008; Hattie, 2009), expertise is not developed based upon the mystical ability of professionals to get it right the first time. Rather, it is based upon the willingness to try techniques, get feedback that is honest, accurate, specific, and timely, and then improve performance.

Thinking Processes

Stanley Pogrow (2009) has been an ardent and thoughtful advocate of HOTS—higher order thinking skills. However, the challenge that vexes teachers (and more than a few parents) is how we distinguish the thinking of students from the decisions that they make. In an algebra problem, this question is of only abstract interest, but in the decision making of teens about drugs, alcohol, and sexual behaviors, it can literally be a matter of life and death. Therefore, it is a matter of more than passing interest that we consider it.

For many students, there is a clear but unstated equivalence between "smart" and "fast"—that is, the really smart kid is not the one who discerns the meaning of *eudemonic* from its cognate roots, but rather the student who memorized it from a spelling list or an *Onion News* video. In fact, however, the ability to reflect on our thinking processes is more important than always having the right answer, no matter how quickly we arrive at it or how accurate it may be. In their landmark research on the subject, W. Chan Kim and Renée Mauborgne (2003) and their colleagues at the European business and leadership school INSEAD learned that decision-making processes are more important than the decisions themselves. This is a strikingly counterintuitive finding, particularly for U.S. citizens who claim to be "bottom-line" oriented. Our rhetoric prefers action and conclusion, but our actual behavior suggests that process, not results alone, is essential. Kim and Mauborgne found that when people disagreed with a decision but understood the process that led to it, they were more satisfied than if they agreed with the decision but found the process mysterious and unfair.

Collaboration, for example, is frequently listed as a desirable 21st century skill. We should consider which grading practices most encourage this trait. Are they the practices that reward only the student who is smart, fast, and competitive, or the practices that encourage the student who is deliberate, overtly thoughtful, and collaborative?

The world recently endured a global economic calamity in which an exclusive focus on the bottom line, the next quarter's earnings, the immediately apparent performance, led to the exclusion of a thoughtful review of process. We have traversed this territory before. For six years before its collapse in 2001, Enron made the list of the "world's most admired companies" and was hailed as an icon of innovation. Fannie Mae was similarly the subject of adulation. Both are bankrupt. Would it have been overly tedious for someone to ask, "We see that the conclusions you have reached are doubtlessly brilliant and that you reached them quickly, but could you say how you reached them?"

In an era of rewards bestowed upon the students who memorize quickly and test well, we would do well to ask this same question. The point is not to embarrass our best students but to give them what they need most—challenge, engagement, and respect. With declining budgets for assessments, more schools and institutions of higher learning will rely upon tests that are cheap and worth the price. It falls to teachers and local educational leaders, therefore, to ask, "Could you explain how you reached those conclusions?"

Behavior

We want people to behave better, whether they are the whiny adolescent in our math class, the screaming baby in the grocery store, the ill-tempered business person in front of us at the airport security line, or the impatient person behind us in traffic. In the context of the classroom and the workplace, one of the most common methods to cope with bad behavior is criticism. "Whining, screaming, huffing, and honking are all ill-considered strategies," we'd like to say—or something like that. Criticism of the behavior of others certainly feels good, but as with the pigeon leaving a deposit on the statue of Lord Nelson in Trafalgar Square, our criticism probably has little impact on the target. Consider just a few of the student behaviors that many teachers wish to modify—inattentiveness, tardiness, incomplete work, and disrespect. One possible strategy to deal with these behaviors is to shout "MATH: B MINUS!" or "HISTORY: C!" or, for especially difficult students, "CHEMISTRY: C MINUS!" In this particular strategy, the link made between behavior and consequence leads directly to the student who responds to the parental query, "How did you get that grade?" with the predictable response, "I dunno."

There is a better way. If we would like students to change their behavior, the first thing we need to do is identify with precision the behavior we wish to change and then decide, as Michael Fullan (2008b) suggests, if the impending battle over behavioral modification is worth fighting for. If the answer is in the affirmative, then let us by all means fight, but let us do so in a manner that has at least some probability of victory. If the school were ablaze and we needed to evacuate the building, no sentient teacher would be shouting "MATH: B MINUS!" She would instead be giving directions that would secure the safety of the students. Therefore, if inattentiveness, tardiness, and disrespect are opponents worth engaging, what are the most effective methods to do so?

Defining Behavior With Clarity

First, define the behavior with absolute clarity. Step aside from the academic realm for a moment, and consider something on which every reader can agree. We want our kids to be healthy, and one important part of their health is that they maintain a reasonable weight relative to their height. So which do we really want—health or ideal weight? Some parents—indeed, some spouses—have engaged in mandatory weigh-ins for their loved ones, focusing only on weight loss, an objective that can be achieved with diet and exercise or, if the incentives are sufficient, with anorexia and drug abuse. The latter course will lead to weight loss, and parents, partners, spouses, boyfriends, and girlfriends who focus exclusively on weight will find themselves disappointed, alone, or both. If, in the context of school behavior, we wish for students to be attentive, punctual, and respectful, then do we assess only their absences, tardiness, and disciplinary records, or do we explore the causes for success and failure in each of these domains? If tardiness is associated with an alcoholic parent who cannot wake up in time to transport a student to school, then a lecture on the value of punctuality is unlikely to be of much help. On the other hand, the opportunity to make up work in a structured time during the day may be useful.

The student, therefore, cannot use the home environment as an excuse for poor performance, but neither is the home environment an academic death sentence. By "defining the behavior," in this case, we indicate to the student that the essential issue is not complying with a school schedule that is incompatible with parental alcohol abuse; rather, the essential issue is getting student work done in a timely and diligent manner. Similarly, I wish that I could say that all of my students walk in the door with the tip of the hat offered to Mr. Chips, the endearing English schoolmaster. The truth is, they don't. Some are plugged into audio distractions, others are focused on their friends, and others are lost in their own thoughts and in preoccupations that I can scarcely understand. There is, however, a middle ground between a contemptuous adjudication of their behavior as disrespectful and the conclusion that they are just kids and therefore incapable of giving their respectful attention.

Respectful attention, particularly to adult instruction, is a skill to be practiced. Even the most disrespectful students can learn to be attentive when the object of their focus is an electronic game. What does the electronic game provide to the disengaged student? Immediate feedback and guidance and incremental opportunities for improvement. If we wish to improve the behavior of students, then the pledge to give them a final failing grade and the exchange of contemptuous glances until, mercifully for both parties, the semester ends, is an unlikely prescription for success. Teachers can improve student behavior by considering the lessons of electronic games—using feedback that is immediate, specific, and incremental.

As in the case of academic performance, a rubric might be useful, creating a 4-point spectrum of performance. For example, teachers wishing to improve levels of student attentiveness might consider some specific opportunities for improvement along a continuum like the following:

1. You are asleep, distracted, conversing with others, playing with electronic devices, or otherwise disengaged from the class. You are showing me that you do not even care about the class, your fellow students, or me as a professional educator.

2. You are pretending to pay attention, but we both know it is only superficial engagement. You look forward and have your book open, but you are not participating actively in individual and group work.

3. You are seated when the bell rings and have your book and papers ready. You volunteer to participate in class and group activities. You ask questions and contribute actively to class discussions.

4. You take an active leadership role in the class, noticing when other students need help and encouragement. You regard it as a personal mission to help other students move from "level 1" to higher levels of engagement that you know will lead to better success for the entire class.

In sum, if our objective is to improve student behavior, then our first obligation as teachers and leaders is to describe with clarity and specificity the behavior that we wish to achieve. Rewards and punishments are insufficient, as we will consider in the next few paragraphs. We must know what we want and describe it with precision.

Using Incentives Correctly

There is a rich psychological literature about the relative impact of rewards and punishments. As Daniel Pink (2009) and Alfie Kohn (1999) demonstrate, rewards can be misused. Rewards render students dependent upon them and create what cognitive psychologist Daniel Willingham (2009) has called "praise junkies," students who are unable to engage in work without another jolt of the praise drug to their system.

Punishments can be even worse, encouraging students to avoid difficult tasks or modify troublesome behaviors. Students witness the futility of punishment on a regular basis, when teachers insist on the use of grading policies that institutionalize punishment for previous bad behavior. When teachers use the average and zero, for example, the inattention, tardiness, incomplete work, and disrespect of January is punished well into May. If the same teacher departed from an otherwise strict diet with a donut and ice cream binge on New Year's but resumed his regimen in February, March, April, and May, what would matter most is the physical health of the teacher in May. No physician or trainer would say, "I'd give you a clean bill of health and encourage your progress, but I just can't get over that weekend you failed to follow your instructions." If that were the case, we would never engage in the effort to be healthy, emulating the futility and resentment of students who ask, "What does it matter? I can't win. There's nothing I can do. I might as well give up."

Incentive systems, therefore, must provide balanced measures of reinforcement, correction, forgiveness, and resilience. While poor performance must be identified and confronted, let us call it what it is—poor performance, not an immutable character flaw. When we wish students to pay attention, we can help them practice the essential skill of focus (Gallagher, 2009), but we need not assume that inattention was due to their contempt for our favorite subject. It is also possible that disengagement was related to disappointment over a relationship, their parents' divorce, the death of a loved one, or another cause that, had it occurred in the life of an adult friend, would have been perfectly understandable.

Rewards and punishment will, when administered with absolute consistency, help a lab rat find its way through a maze. But when these rewards and punishments are administered in a haphazard manner, they will drive the same lab rats insane (Lehrer, 2009). In fact, the frustrated lab animal will starve to death rather than pursue a reward that is easily accessible if that reward appears to be inconsistent and unfair, accessible one moment and beyond reach the next.

When it comes to students, we cannot improve behavior with a simple combination of rewards and punishments. High and low grades, honor rolls, detentions, and the host of other recognitions and humiliations that are regularly used in schools are of little value unless the incentives they seek to provide are clear to the students. Ironically, even the best incentive systems sometimes lead to cynicism rather than commitment, an attitude diametrically opposed to what teachers attempt to instill in students.

Integrity

"I'd like to have your locker combination," I said in terse but measured tones to Sarah, a student I had caught red-handed plagiarizing. "Why?" Sarah asked, responsive, but not submissive. "Because," I said with honest intensity, "I would like to steal your stuff. I'd like to take your CDs, skateboard, pictures, books, and anything else I want."

After a pause, during which Sarah had to choose between the absurdity of my demand and the seriousness of my demeanor, she finally asked, "Why? Why do you want my stuff?"

"Because," I replied, "you thought it was okay to steal from someone else, so I thought you wouldn't mind if I stole some of your stuff."

"I didn't ever steal anybody's stuff," Sarah said defensively. "That's not right, and you have bad information. I never steal."

I then presented her paper to her. It was the text of a four-minute speech, which was, word for word, copied from a popular student website to which I subscribe and for which I pay an annual fee. Next to her paper, I provided my download from the site. "Of course you steal," I said. "These words are not your words. You stole them."

This is not a morality tale that has a happily-ever-after ending. Sarah was indignant. She believed with sincerity that she had done nothing wrong. She was an honor roll student, normally immune from and indifferent to the criticism of faculty members. She had school figured out and understood what she had to do in order to earn good grades, avoid uncomfortable confrontations, and get out of her small town. One thing she had to do in order to earn good grades was copy the work of others. It was hardly a moral dilemma. Her older siblings copied music every day from the Internet, explaining that only suckers paid for music and that iTunes was for fools. Her parents sang in a church choir, following carefully the score emblazoned with an imprint that said "Do Not Copy," while the director reasoned that violation of copyright law in service of a deity was acceptable.

What about Sarah? If she were the daughter of the school-board chair, her violation might be viewed as a youthful mistake; if she were the child of an unemployed single mother, her breach of integrity could lead to a course failure, expulsion, and a mark on her transcript that would label her forever as a failure and a cheat.

What if Sarah were your child? Surely you would not condone plagiarism, but neither would you expect that she should receive academic corporal punishment for her bad judgment. You might even acknowledge that you, as a parent, had some role in Sarah's flawed decision making. Remember, Sarah did not fail to turn in work—the consequence for which is almost always a zero. She did not turn in the work late, the consequence for which is frequently at least a reduction in the final score by one grade. She did not fail to work—she actually worked very hard, scanning several websites to find the perfect place to copy, cheat, and plagiarize her way into the honor roll. There are several alternatives to consider.

The first, and most commonly used consequence, is reward. That's right—we talk a good game about academic integrity, but we reward plagiarism routinely. In one case of blatant plagiarism, the "punishment" was a reduction in grade from A to B, and even this consequence was greeted with protest by the student and parents. Another consequence is academic capital punishment, including expulsion, transcript notices, or other marks of iniquity that might as well be a scarlet letter on the forehead of the offender. Perhaps a better consequence is the invasion of the locker, a consequence that contemporary students understand: "I will ransack your Sababa CDs, I will tear up your boyfriend's letter, and I will destroy your diary." These are, to most teenagers, far more serious consequences than suspension, expulsion, or reductions in letter grades. My students are good kids who have a decent moral compass, but they have reached their late teenage years without a clue as to what plagiarism is, without a sense of what integrity means, and without a well-developed notion of empathy. When I tell them, "If you steal words, it's the same as if I take stuff out of your locker," there is a long pause, and the lights go on.

Our goal in this chapter has been to improve the specificity of grading. If we wish to improve academic performance, attitude, integrity, or any other element of performance, we must be clear and specific about our expectations. In the next chapter, we will look at the element of timeliness in grading.

Chapter 6

HOW TO IMPROVE
TIMELINESS

Feedback, when it is accurate, fair, specific, and timely, has a profound impact on student achievement. In fact, as we have seen, quality feedback can have a greater influence than family and socioeconomic factors on student results. Because grades are among the most important feedback that students receive, it is particularly important that students receive information about their academic performance in a timely manner. In this chapter, we explore how educators can improve the speed with which they provide feedback to students.

Jeff Howard is the founder of the Efficacy Institute, an organization with a more than two-decade track record of dramatic improvements in the performance of high-poverty urban schools. Howard (personal communication, May 5, 2010) wondered how urban students could be several years behind their peers in proficiency in reading and math yet able to master very quickly the complex knowledge and skills required to obliterate space aliens from a computer screen. The ability to become masters of the virtual universe, Howard observed, was not a matter of blasting away mindlessly at an imaginary enemy. There were a complicated series of moves, often with multiple steps and complex contingencies, that players had to use in order to succeed, in the parlance of gamers, at the "next level" of competition. It just didn't make sense, he concluded, that students could do ten-step problem solving with an electronic game but were adjudged to be incapable of solving two-step equations in middle school.

The lessons that Howard learned and applied successfully in some of the nation's most challenging schools are the focus of this chapter. Howard called his insight "the Nintendo Effect," referring to the dramatic improvement in performance that students are capable of demonstrating when they receive feedback that is immediate and when they have an opportunity to use that feedback to improve their performance.

Why Timely Feedback Is So Important

The television drama *House* is engaging, because the cranky physician who is the lead in the eponymously named series learns the elusive diagnosis just in time to save the patient. There is drama, because the patient might die, and the fiction is credible because many viewers have had experiences, or know of friends or family members with experiences, that resonate with the plot of each episode. "We had a symptom that we thought was one diagnosis, but it was something else. We were not hypochondriacs after all, but had a real disease. Take that," we say, to the doubting family member, friend, or colleague at work. "We were not slacking, but were really sick. We might have died! Thank goodness for Dr. House." House reveals his insights in a series of connections and flashbacks that leave his viewers amazed. His crankiness is forgiven, because after all, genius excuses rudeness.

The real world, it turns out, has some eerie similarities to this television series, both in the close calls where timely feedback is necessary to save lives and in the catastrophic consequences that ensue when feedback, however technologically sophisticated and expert, is too late to be of value. Atul Gawande is a surgeon in Boston and the author, most recently, of *The Checklist Manifesto* (2009). Gawande also leads the World Health Organization's Safe Surgery Saves Lives program and is the recipient of a MacArthur fellowship. With certifiable genius and advanced expertise in an exceptionally technical field, Gawande might be expected to offer complex solutions to the complex challenges of surgery and critical care in the 21st century. What he provides instead, however, is bound to disappoint those who are held in thrall by the mystery of expertise. Dr. Gawande, who is a real genius and does not just play one on television, offers only a boring checklist. His prospects for starring on a television series may be limited, but one thing is certain: he has saved more lives in a week than Dr. House will in his career, and his insights will continue to do so.

Gawande's secret is the absence of secrecy. By demystifying medical treatment and showing with overwhelming evidence that even extensively trained experts would have superior results if they used checklists, he has helped to reduce hospital death rates, infection frequency, and length of stays in the intensive care unit by orders of magnitude that, as we will see, have staggering implications.

The Surgeon in the Classroom

How are classroom teachers like surgeons? Both see a variety of new and unexpected complications every day. Both deal with factors—nutrition, parental behavior, sleep, just to name a few—that can ameliorate or aggravate the conditions of their patients or students, as the case may be, and both have little or no control over those factors. The breadth and depth of complexity in both cases are stunning. Gawande (2009) explains:

> A study of forty-one thousand trauma patients in the state of Pennsylvania—just trauma patients—found that they had 1,224 different injury-related diagnoses in 32,261 unique combinations. That's like having 32,261 kinds of airplanes to land. Mapping out the proper steps for every case is not possible, and physicians have been skeptical that a piece of paper with a bunch of little boxes would improve matters. (p. 35)

A teacher, particularly in a highly complex school with a transient student population where students speak dozens of different languages at home, suffer from scores of psychological and physiological afflictions, and span perhaps six different grade levels of performance when they enter the classroom, might describe Gawande's dilemma as "a normal day's work." Teachers, like surgeons, resist and resent the idea that their complex tasks can be systematized. It is, they argue, more art than science, and checklists are crafted by those who are more apt to give advice than take it. I share this disbelief, but occasionally my cynicism must give way to the evidence. Here are a few of the findings in Gawande's (2009) exploration of the virtues of checklists in the medical context:

- Reduced line-infection rates from 11 percent to zero
- Prevented forty-three infections and eight deaths and saved two million dollars in costs—all in a single hospital

- Reduced from 41 percent to 3 percent the likelihood of a patient's enduring untreated pain

- Reduced the proportion of patients not receiving the recommended care by a quarter; twenty-one fewer patients died than in the previous year

- Improved the consistency of care to the point that the average length of patient stay in intensive care dropped by half

Note well that the results are not perfect. Doctors still make mistakes, and patients still die. But feedback—particularly when it is provided in a timely way, reduces the impact of those mistakes in a substantial way. How can we apply this to schools? First, we must acknowledge that the standard for consideration of improved practice is not perfection but improvement. I have presented evidence of how improved feedback policies can, for example, improve homework compliance, reduce unexcused absences, and decrease the failure rate (Reeves, 2009b). Surprisingly, a frequent response to these findings is not, "Thanks—that will make next year a lot better," but rather "You haven't seen *my* students—I know of some kids who will just *never* do the work, will *never* show up, and will *never* respond to feedback."

Accepting, for the sake of argument, that these unnamed students are doomed, resistant to any intervention the teacher might offer, their existence should not prevent us from pursuing the greatest improvement for the greatest number of students. The fact that some patients die of infection despite our best efforts does not relieve physicians from the burden of washing their hands, sanitizing the operating arena, and covering their mouths with a surgical mask. If we can ask people with a dozen years of postgraduate medical training to use checklists in order to gain immediate feedback on their practice and make appropriate midcourse corrections, then we can and must ask teachers and school administrators to do the same.

Standards of Timeliness

How timely must our feedback be? In the case of the hospital emergency room, timeliness is measured in seconds and minutes. In the case of something really important, such as playing an electronic game, the feedback loop is even shorter. What about the feedback for teachers, educational leaders, and students? In most school systems, the most important feedback—the data that will lead to evaluation, reward, and sanctions for teachers and administrators, and that may determine the opportunities for students—is separated from the performance by months. Teachers are routinely summoned to data analysis meetings in which they are required to analyze data on students who are no longer in their classroom. Dr. House's audience would surely decline if he descended into a Kafkaesque world in which each episode was an exploration of the maladies of the patient who was featured in the previous week's story—especially if the patient had already died.

Fortunately, we have standards of timeliness that are accessible to almost every school. Just as an emergency room seeks to assess one hundred percent of patients in a timely manner and provide care for them that is appropriate to their needs, so also a classroom teacher can seek to meet the same standard. Watch a great music teacher in action—within minutes, the chorus, band, or orchestra is ready to perform, and the teacher is providing feedback to each of the students on how to improve. Watch a great athletic coach—students do not wait for instruction, but take to the field or floor or ice, shooting baskets, practicing shots, and receiving feedback not just from the coaches but from other students. Can this be applied to the classroom?

In Harlem Village Academy, mathematics classes begin the day with a five-item quiz. Students and teachers know within the first few minutes of class exactly what students know, where they should focus, and how they can improve. At schools around the world, students and teachers use *The Art of Teaching Writing*, by Lucy Calkins (1994). Calkins helps students provide feedback to one another, so that every few minutes of every class students write, read the writing of their fellow students, and give and receive feedback.

When I taught graduate courses in assessment and research, I would take my students on a field trip to watch a school basketball game coached by Craig Ross. My students would record the following observations:

- The percentage of players who received feedback

- The frequency of feedback for each player
- The nature of the feedback—negative, positive, prescriptive, challenging
- The impact of the feedback—that is, did the feedback lead to improved performance?

The results were not particularly remarkable, at least in the context of a basketball game:

- One hundred percent of the players received feedback.
- Within a single fifteen-minute quarter, each player typically received feedback between five and fifteen times, the variation depending on the needs of the player.
- The nature of the feedback was widely variable. The coach knew that some students needed constant reinforcement, others needed to be challenged, others needed to be reminded specifically of what to do, and others needed to be asked to think about how to respond to a particular challenge. The coach (now the very successful chief executive officer of a global corporation) seemed to understand that different students needed different sorts of feedback, though I'm certain that we never breathed the words *differentiated instruction.*
- The impact of the feedback was clear—we were a small school with no scholarships, and no one enrolled there because of the basketball program. Yet we beat teams that were bigger, stronger, taller, and better. Our teacher—our coach—never yelled, cursed, and labeled his students, but he gave them feedback that led directly to improved performance.

I then challenged my students to make the same observations in a class at school. The contrast was striking:

- How many students received feedback? Typically, there was positive feedback for the eager few who raised their hands and volunteered and negative feedback for the other extreme, the few students who were disruptive. For the vast quiet middle, there was little or no feedback, as if we had made a bargain with them—"Don't bother the teacher, and the teacher won't bother you."

- What was the frequency of feedback? It was, in the terms of our research class, a skewed distribution, with most feedback going to a few students.

- What was the nature of the feedback? It was almost entirely binary—great/awful, wonderful/wretched, right/wrong.

- What was the impact of the feedback? It was difficult to tell, because there was no score keeping that was in evidence aside from the invisible good and bad marks by the teacher and the inevitability of a report card nine weeks hence.

Craig was an excellent coach and teacher, but his techniques did not need to be exceptional. Providing feedback in every class—even in every "quarter" of every class—is not an impossible standard. Providing feedback that is specific and differentiated and that influences student results is a realistic expectation. We only need to take math, science, social studies, English, and every other discipline as seriously as we take basketball.

How Teachers Can Improve Timeliness

Teachers can accelerate the pace of feedback to students in three ways: (1) by involving students in establishing academic criteria, (2) by using a three-column rubric, and (3) by offering midcourse corrections.

Involve Students in Establishing Academic Criteria

The fastest feedback a teacher can possibly provide to a student is feedback that takes place before the teacher ever even sees the student work product.

How can that happen? In *Student-Generated Rubrics*, Ainsworth and Christinson (1998) demonstrate the advantages in terms of clarity and timeliness that occur when students have a hand in creating and applying scoring rubrics in the classroom. Involving students in the creation of criteria for academic performance can be threatening to some teachers; after all, *we* are the teachers, and our expertise is obviously greater than that of our students. While that assumption is generally true, we might be surprised at the level of sophistication and clarity with which students are able to define different levels of performance in an academic context. Listen, for example, when students explain the rules of a game on the playground: "You can go here, but you can't go there." "You can do this, but you can't do that, but if you see someone else do this, then you get to do that." It's a whole series of complex and conditional rules. The same is true of the precision with which students are able to describe how to do everything from play an electronic game to survive in the social network of middle school. Once they know the rules of the game, they can evaluate their own performance and that of others, and they can improve at a rapid pace. If they don't know the rules of the game, or if the rules of the game are subject to sudden and unannounced changes—middle school social networks again come to mind—then we sadly observe the result: students simply stop playing the game.

So it is with academic work. Once a student concludes that "I'm just not a good writer" or "I'll never get math," then it becomes strikingly more difficult to restore that student's confidence. Such students have a fixed mindset (Dweck, 2006). They have become dependent upon the feedback of teachers to affirm their performance, because they have not developed the ability to accurately assess their own work. The result, even among high-achieving students, can be damaging. University of Virginia psychological researcher Daniel Willingham (2009) warns of the perils of praise when students crave the adulation of teachers more than the satisfaction of having done a task well. Thus, scoring rubrics that are created and applied by teachers not only save time and accelerate feedback, but also build students' analytical insight and confidence.

Use the Three-Column Rubric

The second way for teachers to improve timeliness is the three-column rubric, with one column for performance criteria, a second column for student self-assessment, and a third for teacher assessment. In many more advanced tasks, student-generated rubrics may not be appropriate, as the teacher must use experience, judgment, and expertise to create the rubric. Nevertheless, we can express the performance criteria in language that can be used by the vast majority of students. When the teacher creates the first column of criteria in advance of the work, the student completes the second column before the work is submitted; the teacher need only focus on the third column—those specific performance criteria for which the teacher's assessment of performance differs from the student's.

This technique avoids the repetition of obvious corrections and, most importantly, removes the teacher from serving in the "factory foreman" role, in which the student is the benighted laborer, unaware of the quality of the work he or she has done without inspection by a manager. When the teacher provides feedback only on those areas where the teacher's assessment varies from the student's self-assessment, the teacher is able to differentiate feedback for each student explicitly according to the needs of that student. Moreover, the teacher is providing fewer comments for each student and focusing them in areas that will have the greatest impact on student performance. I have used this technique with students ranging from primary grades to graduate school, and I have found that it saves hours every week compared to my previous technique of providing laborious written feedback on every assignment. Much like the checklists that Gawande (2009) found useful in a variety of settings, the student's self-assessment provides a shortcut that avoids a great deal of the mechanical and low-level feedback from teacher to student. An example of a three-column rubric appears in figure 6.1 (page 88).

Offer Midcourse Corrections

The third way for teachers to improve the timeliness of feedback is to create midcourse corrections for students before the completion of a project. This is particularly useful in major tasks, such as an elementary or secondary school research project. One of the least efficient work processes in schools is the simultaneous submission of major projects on the same day to a teacher who, even with heroic efforts, including nights and weekends devoted to grading, returns the projects weeks after the students submit them. While I deeply respect the time and attention that teachers devote to evaluating and commenting on these projects, there is one unequivocal rule of

Scoring Guide	Student Assessment	Teacher Assessment
1. Organization	1.1 My outline included two levels of structure, including Roman numerals and letters. 1.2 My outline matches the content of my written and oral presentation. 1.3 My outline follows a logical progression, with facts to support my arguments.	*1.3 I don't understand why global warming leads to famine in Africa—could you please elaborate on this?*
2. Research	2.1 I have both primary and secondary sources. 2.2 All of my sources are listed in the references. 2.3 My references include citations from both the Internet and books or periodicals.	
3. Written Arguments	3.1 My written presentation follows the outline structure. 3.2 Each sentence is complete, grammatically correct, and every word is spelled correctly. 3.3 Each section of my paper flows logically to the next, and every paragraph has a logical transition to the next paragraph.	*3.2 Your writing is excellent! Please see the places where I circled incomplete sentences, and rewrite them for the final draft.* *3.3 Please reword the last sentence in the middle paragraph of page 3—I don't understand how it leads to the next section.*
4. Graphics	4.1 I have at least three graphs, charts, or figures to illustrate my main points. 4.2 Each graph is explained in the text.	
5. Oral Presentation	5.1 My presentation opens with a compelling story, statistic, or question. 5.2 My presentation explains the ideas in my paper in a clear and logical way. 5.3 My presentation closes with a provocative question or statement that makes my listeners want to learn more.	*5.1 VERY interesting—you hooked me!* *5.3 I understand your conclusion, but why should I learn more?*

Figure 6.1: Sample three-column scoring rubric.

feedback that applies here: if students do not ever read the feedback, the probability that it will be used to improve performance is zero. Teachers resent the workload, parents complain about dilatory grading, and students have consigned last week's work to the same brain region occupied by the Ice Age—they are vaguely aware of it, but it has little relevance to their academic life.

There's got to be a better way. Midcourse corrections allow teachers to provide differentiated feedback from the beginning of an assignment to the end, identifying and highlighting problems before they begin. A major project might take place over six weeks, which is thirty classroom days on a regular schedule or fifteen classroom days on a block schedule. By allocating ten minutes for two individual check-ins for a regular class of fifty minutes, or twenty minutes for four check-ins during a ninety-minute block, the teacher has created sixty individualized opportunities for review and feedback before the project is due.

Some students might require more frequent progress checks than others. Figure 6.2 (page 90) illustrates how a teacher might provide weekly feedback for students whose history suggests that they need particular help in organization and time management, and less frequent feedback to other students. Note that this structured intermediate feedback differs significantly from the well-intentioned offer to "come see me whenever you need help." In fact, students who most need help do not routinely ask for it. Intervention and assistance must be structured. If we expect students to learn the critical school-survival skill of seeking assistance and getting timely feedback, then we must teach it to them. Teachers are busy.

With class sizes increasing and the burdens for coverage expanding, even while school days are shrinking, it is difficult to imagine devoting time to individual students. Yet it can be done. Students 1, 2, 3, 4, and 5 in figure 6.2 received more frequent feedback than their peers, and the comments in the right-hand column suggest why. They are disorganized, unfocused, and resistant to getting the assignment completed. More timely feedback—ten minutes per period was devoted to differentiated feedback—did not transform these students into paragons of organization and scholarship, but it did allow student and teacher to collaborate in a way that averted the disaster and failure so often associated with long-term projects. By the time students, parents, and teachers know that there is a problem, it is too late to correct it. Differentiated feedback, by contrast, provides for midcourse corrections by the students and opportunities for the teacher to intervene where appropriate.

Day	Students	Sample Comments
Monday	1, 2	1—Outline not started; 2—Topic not selected
Tuesday	3, 4	3—Lost rubric; 4—Loves topic but overwhelmed
Wednesday	5, 6	5—Needs focus; 6—Detailed outline; ready to go
Thursday	10, 11	10—Very advanced; needs challenge beyond "4"
Friday	12, 13	13—Potentially inappropriate topic; check with parents
Monday	1, 2	1—Outline incomplete; 2—Topic too general
Tuesday	3, 4	3—Folder set up, ready to start; 4—Has good focus
Wednesday	5, 7	5—Clear question; needs step-by-step help
Thursday	14, 15	14—Needs help on primary/secondary source difference
Friday	16, 17	17—Ahead of schedule; completely self-directed
Monday	1, 2	1—Wants new topic—no—complete commitment
Tuesday	3, 4	4—Worked through small steps; much better
Wednesday	5, 8	5—Wants to do personal interviews; excellent
Thursday	18, 19	18—Potential plagiarism; warning and explanation
Friday	20, 21	21—Hasn't started; parents divorcing, needs counseling
Monday	1, 2	1—Changed his mind; loves the topic, has first draft!
Tuesday	3, 4	3—Working the checklist; may not finish on time
Wednesday	5, 9	5—Field notes are a mess; needs organizational system

Day	Students	Sample Comments
Thursday	22, 23	23—Exceptional work; almost done
Friday	24, 25	25—Unfocused; did paper before outline; refocus now!
Monday	1, 2	2—Good focus; first draft needs work
Tuesday	3, 4	3—Coordinated with social studies; same topic for both classes; loves the idea
Wednesday	5, 9	5—Organized notes into categories; must write draft
Thursday	26, 27	27—Wants to have web-based appendix; OK
Friday	28, 29	29—Created interactive game; I need to learn more
Monday	1, 2	1—Needs at least one more draft, but will finish
Tuesday	3, 4	3—Rough, but is going to make it
Wednesday	5, 9	5—Draft is on Hunter S. Thompson; needs coherence
Thursday	30, 31	31—Thoughtful, challenging work
Friday	32, 33	33—OK; just going through the motions, not to capacity

Figure 6.2: Differentiated feedback for a major six-week project (35 students).

How School Administrators Can Improve Timeliness

Many schools are using what they call "formative assessments" that may or may not be worthy of the name. As W. J. Popham (2008) and Robert Marzano (2009) remind us, assessments are not formative because of the label, but because teachers use them to inform instruction. Different schools in the same system might be using the same assessments, labeled "formative" or "benchmark" or "interim," but the interpretation and application of those assessment results depend largely on the way in which the school administration creates time for teachers.

In one school, there is time allocated for the administration of the assessment, after which teachers sigh, "Thank goodness that's over—now we can get back to what we were doing." The results, if they are transmitted to teachers at all, arrive weeks later, after teachers and students have already moved on to new units of study.

In another school, administrators are aware of the need for the application of formative assessment data and have allocated time and resources for the analysis and application of such data, as well as for professional learning. Teachers in this school have an intellectual understanding of the value of formative assessment and data analysis, but in the context of a formal class, it remains an abstract notion.

In a third school, however, formative assessment and data analysis are at the heart of weekly professional learning community meetings. "It's just the way we do business," explained Whittier, California, superintendent Sandra Thorstenson (personal communication, August 5, 2009):

> Even if the district takes weeks to give us the final analysis, we keep copies of the formative assessments and evaluate them collaboratively, and students have feedback the very next day on where they did well and how they can improve. As a staff, we know immediately what worked and what didn't, and the exact steps we need to take to be better teachers and leaders.

Although educational leaders sometimes bewail their lack of influence on what happens inside the classroom, there is a great deal that they can do to influence in profound ways the timely use of feedback for improving student results.

Consider Practical Trade-Offs

School leaders should consider some practical trade-offs in making the commitment to timely feedback. First, they must ensure that assessments are focused and brief. School leaders will hear a different view from assessment experts, who will say that in order to sample a content domain adequately, a test should include five or six items per content area. This is a reasonable statement if the purpose of the test is to determine with statistical precision the knowledge of a student about a specific area of academic content. However, the practical impact of this standard is that assessments will include fifty to sixty items for ten or twelve content areas, and the test may therefore require up to two hours of class time.

Assessments must also be administered within a reasonable period of time—twenty to thirty minutes—and the feedback to students and teachers must be immediate, within one or two days. The best practices I have observed involve scoring of periodic assessments the same day, so that teachers have the results, analyzed by subject area and student, immediately enabling teachers and students to apply feedback on performance the next day.

The practical realities of educational leadership are that we must make choices. We simply cannot teach and assess every academic standard, as the illusion of doing so would require more days and hours than are allocated to any school (Marzano & Kendall, 1998). Instead, teachers and leaders must embrace power standards (Ainsworth, 2003), that subset of standards that have the greatest impact on student achievement—assessments that are brief, focused, and provide immediate feedback for students and teachers. The risk, of course, is that this emphasis on brevity will fail to analyze fully student understanding of a subject, and therefore leaders must choose wisely among the available options. On the one hand, an assessment might be so long and comprehensive that its results are delivered late to the teacher and not used by the student. On the other hand, an assessment that is too short underestimates the proficiency of the student. Both lead to error, but the second risk is far better than the first.

Create Time to Analyze and Make Use of Feedback

The second obligation of educational leaders is to create time for teachers to analyze and use feedback. The best practice is when formative assessment for students is accompanied by an early dismissal the same day or a late start the next, so that teachers can meet together, score the assessments collaboratively, and plan appropriate instructional interventions and enrichments. Every school has faculty meeting and professional development meeting times built into the schedule; the central question for the leader is how this time is used. If leaders wish to focus professional learning on student achievement, then they make a deliberate choice to give up traditional meetings, announcements, and workshops, and replace those activities with a clear and explicit focus on student learning. There is no extra time in the day of a teacher or school leader. Every minute devoted to administrative announcements is a minute that cannot be devoted to the analysis of student learning; every minute wasted on death by PowerPoint is a minute that cannot be invested in a review of the most recent formative assessment data. Leaders must, in brief, not only decide what they wish to do but also what they will not do.

Monitor Teacher Responses

The third obligation of educational leaders is to monitor the *response* of teachers to student achievement data. Note well: this is dramatically different from the prevailing fear of teachers that they will be evaluated based upon student data. "If my students do not perform well on tests, then I might get fired" is representative of the prevailing feeling of teachers who oppose the use of data in schools. Therefore, leaders must be explicit about how they explain the relationship of data and evaluation: no teacher is ever evaluated based upon student test scores, but we are all evaluated based upon how we respond to those scores.

Think of it this way: physicians are not evaluated based upon the illnesses of patients who come to the hospital. Of course they are sick—that's why they came to the hospital. However, it is very reasonable to hold physicians at least partly accountable for what happens to the patients *after* they come to the hospital. If they are ill, for example, but hospital-borne infections make them even more ill, then hospitals should be held accountable. Similarly, if students arrive at school two grades behind grade level in reading, that is not the fault of teachers or administrators. However, if we fail to respond to that information—fail to give them more time on literacy and other appropriate interventions—then we become responsible for the failures of that child. This is the critical distinction for leaders—we are not responsible for the initial data about the student, but we do bear ultimate responsibility for our response to that data.

In this chapter we looked at the element of timeliness in grading and at the practices teachers can use to deliver feedback in a timely way. In the next chapter, we will look at how to support timeliness by examining strategies teachers can use when grading.

Chapter 7

TIME-SAVING STRATEGIES FOR BUSY TEACHERS

In this chapter, we will consider how effective grading strategies save time for busy teachers. First, we challenge the notion that traditional grading policies are as efficient as they appear. In fact, grading systems that lead to higher levels of student failure not only have enormous costs for the student in terms of frustration and academic distress, but also cost teachers and schools excessive time and energy. By contrast, effective grading systems save time and are therefore in the best interests of both students and teachers. In particular, we will consider the menu system, a grading system that I have used with students ranging from elementary to graduate school. This represents one of many possible ways that teachers can save time and also provide feedback to students in a way that is accurate, fair, and specific.

"We Don't Have the *Time!*"

Any new policy, whether it has to do with grading, curriculum, assessment, discipline, or any other educational issue, will not have a prayer of implementation if it attempts to cram additional tasks into the days of teachers who are already overwhelmed with initiatives. In a national study, University of Pennsylvania researchers Richard Ingersoll and David Perda (2009) found that, contrary to many stereotypes about teacher dissatisfaction (inadequate pay, poor discipline, standardized testing, and so on), the greatest source of dissatisfaction was the lack of time to do their jobs well.

In fact, many grading reforms are stopped in their tracks, because teachers assume that any policy that encourages students to do more and better work will, as a consequence, require more time and work from the teacher. Consider the case of alternative consequences for missing work. When a student fails to complete a homework assignment, the fastest thing for a teacher to do is enter a zero in the gradebook. In the stroke of a pen or the click of a mouse button, the grading of that particular student assignment is completed. That's about as fast as grading gets, isn't it?

Considered in isolation, this does seem fast, but as many readers of this book know, this is a false comparison, because for each zero we enter in the gradebook, there are at least four very time-consuming consequences that may result:

1. A student who accumulated zeroes will eventually learn—perhaps through a warning letter sent to parents—that he or she is in trouble and ask the teacher for help. The vast majority of teachers will offer this help—often before school, during breaks, or after school. During those conferences, the "quick" zero doesn't appear to be such a time-saving strategy.

2. The student will fail, and the teacher will suffer through the remainder of the academic term with an angry, unmotivated, disengaged, and perhaps disruptive student.

3. After a course failure, the teacher may see the same student again to repeat the same class the following year. Consider your own experience with students who are repeating a class. What is the relative amount of emotional energy and time that they require to get through the class, compared to students who are engaged and motivated?

4. Zeroes and the failures that accompany them can lead to overly drawn-out discussions with parents and administrators.

Alternatives to the "Quick" Zero

What is the alternative to the quick zero? Two positive alternatives can save time and improve student performance. First, teachers can change the consequences for missing work from a zero to the requirement that students complete the work: "Randall, it appears that you've made a choice today to sit at the quiet table at lunch and complete your homework." There are many variations on this theme. In elementary schools, some teachers build in fifteen to twenty minutes of unstructured time in which freedom of choice is earned. Students who choose not to do assigned work when it is due have, by default, chosen to lose that freedom, and must use the time that might have been unstructured to complete their work. For secondary-school students, there are many times during the day—during homework, academic advisories, study halls, X blocks, lunch, and structured interventions before and after school—that can be used as an immediate and appropriate consequence for missing work.

Does it work for everyone? Certainly not, but it works for a surprisingly large number of students. In one comprehensive high school, this reform, as part of a comprehensive intervention and communication plan for students who were failing, resulted in more than one thousand fewer course failures in a high school of about three thousand students (Reeves, 2006b, 2008a). Because reduced failures led to significant improvements in discipline and suspensions, teachers reported saving a great deal of time that they did not have to devote to student behavioral issues.

A second time-saving strategy is the use of a "menu system" for students. When students set learning goals and are able to track them in a clear and meaningful way, their achievement substantially improves (Marzano, 2007). The menu system allows students to take responsibility for their learning and assume appropriate consequences for missing work. When they fail to complete an assignment or if they do badly on a test, the result is neither excuses by the students nor sympathy from the teacher. Rather, students must take the initiative to choose something else from the menu. Consider the example in figure 7.1 (page 98) from a sixth-grade social studies course.

Student Name: _____ **Period #** _____

In this class, 900 points are required to earn an A, and 800 points are required to earn a B. You must work sufficiently hard to earn one of those two grades. For each assignment, project, and assessment, you will have a scoring rubric that includes ratings of exemplary, proficient, progressing, and not meeting standards. As you will see below, you will earn credit only for work that is completed at the exemplary and proficient levels. If your work is not at least proficient, then please work harder, and ask for assistance.

Our focus this quarter is colonial America. You must choose at least one assignment within each major category—government, geography, economics, and culture. Otherwise, you may choose any combination from the menu to earn points for the grade you wish to achieve.

1. Government

1.1 Research project (300 points for exemplary, 240 points for progressing)

1.2 Book review (100 points for exemplary, 80 points for progressing)

1.3 Article review (50 points for exemplary, 40 points for progressing)

1.4 Electronic game creation (200 points for exemplary, 160 points for progressing)

1.5 Unit tests (100 points for exemplary, 80 points for progressing)

1.6 Concept map of unit test content (50 points for exemplary, 40 points for progressing)

2. Geography

2.1 Research project (300 points for exemplary, 240 points for progressing)

2.2 Book review (100 points for exemplary, 80 points for progressing)

2.3 Article review (50 points for exemplary, 40 points for progressing)

2.4 Electronic game creation (200 points for exemplary, 160 points for progressing)

2.5 Unit tests (100 points for exemplary, 80 points for progressing)

2.6 Concept map of unit test content (50 points for exemplary, 40 points for progressing)

3. Economics

3.1 Research project (300 points for exemplary, 240 points for progressing)

3.2 Book review (100 points for exemplary, 80 points for progressing)

3.3 Article review (50 points for exemplary, 40 points for progressing)

3.4 Electronic game creation (200 points for exemplary, 160 points for progressing)

3.5 Unit tests (100 points for exemplary, 80 points for progressing)

3.6 Concept map of unit test content (50 points for exemplary, 40 points for progressing)

4. Culture

4.1 Research project (300 points for exemplary, 240 points for progressing)

4.2 Book review (100 points for exemplary, 80 points for progressing)

4.3 Article review (50 points for exemplary, 40 points for progressing)

4.4 Electronic game creation (200 points for exemplary, 160 points for progressing)

4.5 Unit tests (100 points for exemplary, 80 points for progressing)

4.6 Concept map of unit test content (50 points for exemplary, 40 points for progressing)

Figure 7.1: Sample menu system for a sixth-grade social studies class.

The Menu System at Work: Matilda and Marquez

Consider how this works in practice with two students, Matilda and Marquez. Matilda struggles with tests, but she is fascinated by electronic games. Although she can read well, she reads slowly, and she learns better when she focuses on information in chunks, rather than attempting to absorb a great deal of content at once. She also responds well to graphic representation of information. Marquez writes for the school newspaper, loves investigating topics, and writes regularly for pleasure. The prospect of research papers is, for him, an opportunity to show the teacher what he does best. Unlike many of his peers, however, he has been alienated from electronic games.

Both students worked hard during this quarter, learning a great deal about government, geography, economics, and culture during colonial times. Matilda took all four tests, scoring after considerable study at the proficient level on three of them and earning 240 points, but she failed to earn points on the fourth. She completed two electronic games at the "exemplary" level, acing the scoring rubric with games that included at least twenty "moves" by the player, with each move having an historically accurate context and consequences. This earned her another 400 points, for a total of 640 points for the quarter. Matilda intended to do a book review, but she was poorly organized and had difficulty putting her thoughts together in a way that would have earned the required points.

Fortunately, Matilda was able to use the content from books, articles, class discussions, and web research to create two excellent concept maps, earning another 100 points and bringing her total to 740—only 60 points away from the first B she would earn since she started school. At the same time, she was discouraged, having failed in her attempt at the book report and, despite studying, not doing well enough on unit tests to earn credit. Ms. Sorenson, the teacher and creator of the menu, could tell that something was troubling Matilda and asked her what was wrong. "I'm so close, but I just don't have time to do a research project, and I don't think that retaking the tests will help," Matilda said.

"Tell me about the activities this quarter in which you learned the most and that you most enjoyed," replied Ms. Sorenson.

"Easy," Matilda replied. "The games—I've got the software down, and I loved cramming interesting facts and unusual consequences for the players. I think the other kids learned a lot, too."

"Well," said the teacher, "If that's what you like and that is how you learn, then why not do another game?"

"But I only need 60 points for a B," said Matilda. "Creating a game is a lot of work!"

"There are no rules here that require you to hope for the minimum possible," said Ms. Sorenson seriously. "If you do your next game with the detail and thought that you invested in your first two games, you'll have—let's see—940 points, and that's a solid A for the quarter."

"But it's a lot of work!" countered Matilda.

"That," said Ms. Sorenson, "is correct. I can't wait to see it."

There is no assured happy ending to this story. Perhaps, as cynics claim, Matilda will give up, knowing that she was close, but finally diverted by other activities that take precedence in the life of a frustrated adolescent who doesn't get much academic direction at home. On the other hand, perhaps the engagement, excitement, and sense of controlling the learning environment created by the assignment menu will allow Matilda to earn the same grade as Marquez. Thanks to lots of experience, excellent reading ability, and homework regimens every night strictly enforced by his parents, this young man will ace his tests, complete at least one research project, and have time left over to create a game, even though it's beyond what he needs for his usual grade of A. The point of the menu is not to make every student do the same work but rather to engage every student in the value of the work ethic, organization, and resilience.

The menu system is not a panacea. Although it is structured so that students must learn something about each of the major curriculum areas for that quarter, the truth is that some students will overinvest time in content they are interested in and underinvest time in topics that bore them. As Ms. Sorenson knows, however, that's precisely what happened when she used her previous regimen of lectures, group activities, worksheets, quizzes, and tests. Sometimes homework compliance was below 40 percent, and if compliance meant actually using homework to learn something, then it might have been in the single digits. The menu liberated the students and teachers to make choices and select learning goals. The range of activities engaged nearly every student, and the rigor of the scoring rubrics caused students to learn deeply about the topics they selected.

Challenges to the Menu System

Teachers often express two concerns about the menu system. The first is, "What if students wait until the last week to turn everything in?" That's a fair concern, and it is not unreasonable to establish deadlines throughout the term. If students miss a deadline, they can still find something else on the menu rather than turn in late work. Of course, the best situation is when students determine that it is in their own best interest to finish work properly and on time; in fact, they can earn an A before the term is over, giving them something that students crave: freedom and control over their own time.

That leads to the second teacher concern—what if students finish their work too early? That is indeed a possibility, particularly for high-performing students who know how to "play school" very well. The challenge for teachers is how to motivate these students beyond simply gaining yet another appearance on the honor roll. That is why choice, engagement, and creativity are all such vital elements of the menu system. Ask teachers if they would be happier to cut the amount of grading that they have to do at the end of the semester, and I think most will be enthusiastic about the menu system.

Documenting Time-Saving Ideas

These are just two of many ideas that can help teachers save time and improve student performance. Teachers and leaders should make a regular practice of identifying, documenting, and sharing time-saving ideas. This is the starting point for any instructional initiative. A new idea, no matter how promising, is doomed to drown in a cesspool of cynicism and distrust if it begins with extra work for teachers and administrators. By contrast, if we begin each new idea by first creating time and space for it to be nurtured and grow, then we have created an environment of credibility, authenticity, and optimism, the essential nutrients of any instructional initiative or leadership.

Chapter 8

LEADING CHANGE FOR EFFECTIVE GRADING PRACTICES

"But who is going to tie the bell on the cat?" So ends the tale of the council of wise mice who were unanimous in their opinion that the threatening cat should have a bell tied around his neck, a solution that all agreed would make sense, save the lives of mice, and not harm the cat. Unfortunately, however thoughtful and rational their deliberations, the mice were unable to move from policy to implementation. Such moves require courage and the willingness to confront risks. So it is with grading policies. Being right is not enough. Having the preponderance of evidence on your side is insufficient. In fact, establishing mathematical certainty is of scant comfort when emotion, righteous indignation, and indifference to evidence are arrayed against you.

The most common question I receive from audiences around the world begins with the phrase, "How do I convince . . . ?" The disappointing answer is that you don't. You do not persuade merely with research, evidence, and logic. The evidence for improved grading systems has been around for almost a century. Rather than mere logic and facts, we need a thoughtful process for implementing policy changes, and that is what this chapter offers. We will first reconsider the fundamental purposes of grading and the criteria for establishing any educational policy. Then we will analyze ways of considering alternatives, and finally we will discuss how to align the entire system to support those policies.

The Purpose of Grading

One of the most perplexing things about debates over grading policy is how very intelligent and rational people can look at the same set of facts and come to radically different conclusions. Perhaps the root cause for this phenomenon is that there are widely differing perspectives on the fundamental purposes of grading. These generally fall into the following categories:

- Giving feedback to students in order to improve their performance

- Reporting to parents on student progress toward specific learning objectives

- Communicating with teachers at the next level of instruction so that they can plan their instruction in a way that will meet a variety of student learning needs

- Giving rewards to students for good behavior and attitudes

- Administering punishments to students for poor behavior and attitudes

- Making public distinctions between good and bad students

While most educators would agree that the first three purposes—feedback, reporting, and communication—are the most important purposes of grading, it does not take very long for most discussions of grading policy to reveal that the last three—rewards, punishment, and distinction—are at the heart of most grading policies. The telltale phrases that reflect this conclusion include the following, paraphrased from many conversations and email exchanges I have had with teachers and school administrators on the subject of grading:

- "I know that she didn't meet the academic standard, but how else am I supposed to recognize that she tried hard, came to class, and finished her homework? Honor roll grades are the only recognition that poor kid will ever get!"

- "He's not even sorry for missing his assignments! His attitude is casual and contemptuous. I don't care if he aced the end-of-course exam—he's failing my class until he shows some contrition." (Contrition is a theme that features prominently with my correspondents who find punitive grading as the last tool available to teachers.)

- "If I let some kids submit their work after correcting it, it's not fair to the other kids who got it right the first time."

Pink (2009) and Kohn (1999) have built strong cases that punishments and rewards, like those used to induce rats to find their way through a maze, are not effective ways to encourage learning. In fact, there is substantial evidence that other variables, including respect, mastery, autonomy, and pursuit of worthy goals, are far more motivating than rewards and punishments. Even when rewards and punishments do influence human behavior, they sometimes have unintended consequences. For example, rewarding teachers for high test scores does not necessarily encourage improved student results, but rather provides a direct incentive for experienced teachers to migrate from poor schools to wealthy ones. Rewarding teachers for growth in test scores—an attempt to induce teachers to stay in poor schools—can unintentionally provide an incentive to focus only on the least mobile students who are right below the level of proficiency. Highly mobile students, or those far below and far above proficiency, need effective teaching too, but if we accept the behavioral theory of reward and punishment, then those students are sacrificed to the prevailing incentive system. These rewards, in other words, miss their targets and fail to achieve their intended results.

The same is true when grades are used as rewards and punishments. Guskey (2000) has marshaled impressive evidence that can be summarized in a single sentence: grading as punishment does not work. In fact, when students are rewarded only with feedback on their performance and are not subjected to a grade, their performance is better than when they are graded. Similarly, when teachers think that they are building work ethic and respect by the use of zeroes for missing work, strict policies against acceptance of resubmission of work, and the use of the average to determine final grades, rather than encouraging work ethic and personal responsibility, they send the following clear message: your semester is over after a few missing assignments, so you might as well give up.

When much of the grade depends upon homework, home projects, and other factors that presume effective parental supervision and a stable home environment, there is another clear message that students receive: you had better be very careful in selecting your parents. If you go home to an attentive and academically encouraging home environment, you will be rewarded. If, on the other hand, you go home to the chaos of unemployment, preoccupation, relocation, or a hundred other social and family dysfunctions, then the impact of those factors on your academic performance and homework completion will be regarded as a sign of laziness, inattentiveness, and inability to complete academic work.

I don't think that the vast majority of teachers would agree that the previous sentences reflect their intentions. If that is the case, then let us proceed to a policy discussion of grading that has as its first principle that *the primary purpose of grading is feedback to students to improve performance.* We should also agree in explicit terms, as a matter of policy, that rewards and punishments for attitudes and behavior, along with the creation of distinctions among students, are not acceptable purposes of grading. Most educators and administrators agree that, when it comes to educational accountability for schools, the primary purpose is the improvement of teaching and learning. They would further agree that it is ineffective and counterproductive to use test scores and accountability policies to rate, rank, sort, humiliate, and publicly rank teachers, administrators, and schools. These same strong beliefs must, therefore, be applied to grading policies.

Implementing Unpopular Policy Changes

Educational leaders must make difficult policy decisions all the time, and in a democracy, one of the criteria for these decisions is the will of a majority of voters. This leads many leaders to make "buy-in" the principal factor that they weigh in establishing educational policy. However, let us take care before we accept this premise. In a recent local election in New Hampshire, for example, the electorate approved, by a three-to-one margin, the installation of a sprinkler system in the elementary school, a decision that brought the school into compliance with state fire code requirements. What if the vote had gone the other way? Are we willing to stipulate that the will of the majority is a value superior to child safety?

Progress in education, from ending segregation to the implementation of evidence-based leadership and teaching practices, has not always been the result of buy-in by staff members or the will of the majority of the electorate. Rather, effective educational change is often the result of visionary leadership that, against all odds and significant resistance, elevates essential values over popularity.

Education is not the only field in which innovation, progress, and change have happened without popular support. In fields as diverse as brain surgery and social work, agriculture and investment banking, prison reform and emergency-room medicine, water purification and the piloting of passenger aircraft, the most consistent pattern for effective change is not the model of buy-in followed by implementation. While change models like buy-in abound, the preponderance of the evidence (Kotter, 1996, 2008) is that they have little impact on consistently creating organizational change. The most obvious public policies—not allowing drivers of trains, planes, and automobiles to use computers while operating life-threatening equipment—are debated, opposed, and delayed. Evidence is not enough, and buy-in is an illusion.

Rather, an emerging consensus in change leadership literature (Heath & Heath, 2010; Gawande, 2009; Patterson et al., 2008; Fullan, 2008a; Deutschman, 2007) suggests a new model for practical change. The missing elements, these authors suggest, include specificity of behavioral change at the individual level. Chip and Dan Heath (2010) suggest, for example, that goals that are too general leave too much for individual interpretation. "Be healthy," to use one example, is not as effective as "drink skim milk." Patterson, Grenny, Maxfield, McMillan, and Switzler (2008) illustrate the same need for specificity in the context of world health, showing how generic programs spent hundreds of millions of dollars, but small behaviorally oriented programs that focused on clear and specific objectives have achieved what mammoth programs could not in preventing disease in developing nations. Gawande's (2009) clarion call for checklists makes clear that even in the most sophisticated professional, corporate, educational, and governmental enterprises, clarity of expectation is at the heart of the new wave of change efforts.

We will now apply this new, four-level, action-oriented change model to implementing changes in grading policy. The same procedure can also be used widely in education. The elements of the model are explicit vision, specification of behavior, assessment and feedback, and continuous refinement.

Explicit Vision

The leader must first create a vivid vision. This is not the gauzy illusion often associated with corporate vision statements, but the vision of an architect who is mobilizing many different people toward a common aim. The vision is clear, specific, and as vivid as the most vibrant painting or sculpture. Do not begin your consideration of grading policy with a generalized discussion about grading policies. That is a procedure that will lead only to hardened positions and commitments to present practice. Rather, begin the discussion with a consideration of student failures and successes. Create two alternative visions, one in which present trends are continued and a second in which there are fewer student failures and more student successes. Let your colleagues brainstorm answers to these questions:

- How would our school be different if we had fewer student failures?

- What would it mean to us if we had fewer students in our classes who were repeating the class for the second or third time?

- If we did not have so many resources diverted to course repetition, what are the new electives that we could offer? What is a course or topic that we have always wanted to teach, but never had time to teach?

- If we had fewer failures, fewer suspensions, fewer expulsions, and even fewer low-level discipline problems, how would our professional and personal lives be better?

We must have a vivid, explicit, and compelling vision in order to ignite difficult changes, whether the challenge at hand is reducing infant mortality, eradicating guinea worm disease, reducing criminal recidivism, or improving student success. Change is too difficult, and reversion to prevailing behavior is too easy, without a compelling vision.

Specification of Behavior

The leader must then create explicit behavioral expectations for implementing the change. Note well that the leader does not say, "I would like you to *believe* in this way," as it is too early in the process to change belief systems. All the leader says is:

> I would like you to do the following things in the following very specific ways. I know that everyone may not agree yet that this is the right course of action, but I want us to try it out, assess our results, and then see if we agree that it was a risk worth taking.

In the context of grading policy, then, the discussion might sound like this:

> We agreed that it is essential for us to reduce course failures, and if we are successful, we will achieve a vision that includes better student success, improved discipline, and a significantly better professional environment for the faculty. In order to achieve that vision, we are making two clear and immediate changes. First, the consequences for missing or low-quality work will no longer be grades of zero or F, but rather a requirement that students complete the work. We will collaborate to create time, support, and appropriate consequences, including time before, during, and after school, for students to finish their work. To be clear, we will no longer use the zero on a 100-point scale. We will no longer use the average to calculate the final grade. Our objective is not to give grades away, but to create an environment in which students earn higher grades and have fewer failures because they worked harder, respected teacher feedback, and completed their work at a higher level of quality than in the past.

Assessment and Feedback

The leader must next assess the implementation of instructional initiatives and identify the level of implementation of the instructional practice and the impact that implementation has on improved student results. It is simply not true that people either implement a policy or fail to implement it. There is, in almost every complex educational matter, a range to successful implementation. When it comes to grading policy, the range might look something like this:

- **Level 1**—The teacher received the research and professional development on grading policy, but there was no implementation in the classroom. There remains evidence of zeroes, averages, and the use of grades to reward and punish student attitudes and behaviors. There is no evidence that low-performing students are using the feedback from grades to improve their performance.

- **Level 2**—Classroom grading policies have been somewhat revised, with late work and revisions to low-quality work accepted, but the prevailing expectation is that work is done only at home. There is little evidence of students using feedback for improved performance.

- **Level 3**—Classroom grading policies meet the school standards, and there is clear evidence of opportunity before, during, and after school for students to improve and complete work. The teacher reports a significant improvement in the quantity and quality of student work, and there is a measurable and significant decline in student failure. Moreover, the improvement in student academic performance is leading to an improved classroom environment.

- **Level 4**—All of level 3 criteria are met, and the teacher has also developed innovative structures to assist underperforming students and to challenge high-achieving students. Moreover, the teacher has innovative structures to encourage higher levels of student performance, improved personal organization, and the timely (or even early) submission of required student work. The teacher is also experimenting with "risk free" assignments in which the sole goal is learning, not the achievement of a grade, and is sharing the promising results of this action research project with colleagues.

This is, of course, only a first draft. Early in any change process, it will be apparent that the change works for some people and does not work for others. Specifications that were crystal clear to the leader were murky to some faculty members. That is why the next level of this change model is necessary.

Continuous Refinement

After assessing the degree of implementation of the change and the impact of those changes on student results, the leader must refine and improve the changes on a continuous basis. The reason for variation in implementation almost always has to do with differences in how various staff members take the same policy, the same training, the same technology tools, and the same leadership guidance and do different things with them. While sometimes there is active resistance that accounts for these differences in implementation, a far more common cause is the failure of leadership to specify with sufficient clarity exactly what change behaviors were expected. In the context of grading, this discussion might sound like this:

> Mr. Walters, in my last visit to the class, I noticed that four students had failed to complete the assignment for the day, but it was not clear to me how you would handle that situation. Could you please explain how the work will be completed and what support from me, if any, you may need to ensure that these students get back on track?

Another conversation might be:

> Ms. Smith, I noticed that to calculate the progress report for your students, you were using the computer default of the average of scores to calculate the grade for your students. I know that the computer does this automatically, but I really trust your judgment about where the student is performing right now, and that is what I would like to see you use not only now, but for the final grades. Can I count on you to do this?

These conversations may strike some readers as focusing on an excessive level of detail, but it is indeed this level of detail that is absent not only in many grading policy improvements but in most areas of change leadership. Leaders undermine their own best intentions time and again when they equivocate. One common temporization goes like this: "The leader is just articulating the vision, but of course each school and classroom teacher will have to determine how best to achieve that vision." This is a prescription for failure, as it suggests that implementation is divorced from goal achievement. What teachers do, from classroom feedback to lesson planning to curriculum articulation to grading policies, is not a matter of personal taste but of effective implementation that requires clarity and specificity. There remain many areas of teacher discretion, such as the engaging scenarios for lessons and assessments, but grading policies or any other educational reform will not achieve improved results if implementation specification is left to chance.

Aligning Systemic Support

Most change initiatives result not in systemic change but in "islands of excellence" (Reeves, 2008b) in which change is demonstrably effective at the individual classroom or school level while systemic change remains elusive. Michael Fullan (2010) makes a compelling case for systems alignment. Because schools and school systems are organizationally complex, change in one part of the system—such as improved grading policy—can have a significant impact on all of the other parts of the system, improving failure rates, discipline, morale, equity, college opportunities, and many other factors. On the other hand, failure to have adequate system alignment will undermine even the most straightforward policy.

Consider the example of teacher and administrator evaluation. Most systems have explicit and implicit evaluation systems. The explicit evaluation systems have little impact on performance (DuFour & Marzano, 2009). They are less likely to be used for termination than lightening is to strike the offending party. Moreover, the evaluation process for both teachers and administrators is a lethargic one, in which feedback occurs long after the instructional and leadership behaviors those evaluations were to influence occurred.

Not only does the explicit evaluation system fail to support change or sanction the failure to change, the implicit evaluation system can actively contradict change messages. Whereas explicit evaluation systems are governed by formal policies and negotiated forms, implicit evaluation systems—the daily conversations among administrators, peers, parents, and other sources of influence—have no such defined boundaries. Any careful observer, however, can identify the prevailing trends in implicit evaluation systems. One of the most common trends is the systemic preference for tranquility and for an absence of conflict and complaint. Therefore, the vociferous complaints of a handful of faculty, parents, administrators, or community members can sometimes be interpreted as "a lot of people are complaining." Because the implicit message is often sent that complaints are bad and the absence of a complaint is good, it is important to establish one essential fact at the outset of any grading policy change: complaints are inevitable, even when your change is successful and student achievement is improving.

When there are fewer failures, many good things happen, including improvements in discipline, achievement, and opportunity. However, improved opportunities for more students to take honor and advanced classes will mean, at least in the short term, that those classes have higher enrollments than they did in the past and that the composition of those classes will be more diverse. Parents (and perhaps a few teachers) who were used to relatively small advanced classes, occupied by students who have traditionally been among the academic elite, may find these changes disconcerting. This becomes a particular problem for leaders when influential and well-connected parents carry their complaints to senior administrative and board of education levels. The immediate priority of an elected official is to "solve the problem" raised by the constituent. The impulsive reaction of the senior administrator is to "avoid a controversy" with a board member, but those reactions, however reasonable and common, are precisely what create tension between the values and goals of the system and the implicit evaluation system and all that it entails.

What can leaders do to achieve better alignment with their implicit evaluation systems? First, they must identify exactly what those implicit messages are and determine whether or not they are congruent with the essential goals of leadership. While elected officials, including members of boards of education, must be sensitive to complaints from constituents, policymaking inevitably involves trade-offs. The pursuit of one goal will diminish the achievement of another, particularly if one of those goals is heavily invested in the preservation of current policies. It is not that leaders and elected officials cannot cope with complaint; my experience suggests, instead, that they prefer to anticipate rather than react to these complaints. When system leaders change policies, they must be alert to potential complaints and let senior administrators and policymakers know what to expect. The response of, "Thanks for your concern—we have actually anticipated that, and here is why we think it's a good idea . . ." is much more protective of stakeholder relationships than a surprised, "Thanks for your concern—I'll have to look into that and get back to you." The latter suggests that there is a problem to be solved; the former suggests that, while the concern may be legitimate, it does not outweigh the other policy priorities that leaders have already considered.

Resolving Disagreements

Of course, not all policy matters are resolved when both sides see the merit of their opposition, withdraw their objections, and live happily ever after. A pluralistic society guarantees diverse points of view. That is its strength, and realistic system leaders acknowledge that the resolution of disagreements is not always a matter of negotiation, mutual concessions, and ultimate agreement. Sometimes, we simply "agree to disagree," and move on in the best interests of the organization.

One of the most important interview questions to ask aspiring administrators, superintendents, and teachers is, "What has happened in the past when you had a disagreement with your colleagues? What were the issues? How did you resolve them? If the issues were not resolved, what did you do?" Although I have asked this question of many candidates, most people are surprised at the inquiry, and even otherwise outstanding candidates dissemble a bit.

The fact is that, particularly in education, we have not done a particularly good job of articulating how we resolve disagreements. The authoritarian "my way or the highway" response is a splendid management philosophy when the building is on fire. Command and control are essential when immediate compliance is required. However there are few—very few—other issues that, in the daily lives of teachers and administrators, rise to the level of "the building is on fire and I need you to do what I'm asking you to do, no questions asked, right now." These are what we might call "safety and value" issues and get to the heart of the first mission of school systems, which is safeguarding the lives—physical, emotional, and intellectual—of the students entrusted to us. When we see adults threaten the lives and well-being of students, whether by throwing a lit cigarette into a wastebasket, striking a child, or engaging in practices that are, on the face of them, destructive, then we have an obligation to stop it. Unfortunately, leaders too rarely distinguish the vital issues worthy of this sort of emotional investment and personal confrontation from other issues. Moreover, because leaders often concentrate their conversation and intellectual energy on their own requirements, they fail to invest similar energy in those areas where they do *not* have mandates and where teachers can exercise professional discretion.

The Three-Level Decision-Making Typology

One effective way of resolving disagreements before they get out of control is the creation of a clear decision-making framework, one that includes those decisions that are within the discretion of the classroom teacher (type 1), those that are subject to collaboration among teachers and administrators (type 2), and those that have been or will be made by senior leadership and must be executed to classroom teachers and building administrators (type 3). In a series of surveys (Reeves, 2006a), I first asked respondents to estimate the percentage of decisions that fell into each category. Not surprisingly, most respondents thought very few decisions fell into the first category, teacher discretion. A few more decisions were collaborative, the respondents speculated. The vast majority of educational decisions, they predicted, were the result of administrative dictates. Then, to get a reality check on these assumptions, I gave the same respondents equal amounts of time to record all of the classroom and school decisions that they could think of for each category. The results were surprising, with more than half the actual decisions falling into the first category of teacher discretion.

Almost 30 percent of the decisions were collaborative, leaving only 20 percent of the actual day-to-day decisions—those that were made in a hierarchical top-down command-and-control manner.

These results were so surprising that many people, including those whose own data contributed to the findings, could barely believe the results. "Everything we do is micromanaged!" they countered. "These results can't be right!" Perhaps you have the same reaction, so rather than argue over whether or not that particular survey applies to you, consider conducting an experiment.

Identify some act of teaching or instructional leadership that, at least on the surface, appears to be uniform. Perhaps it is that, at 9:30 a.m., there should be guided reading in every second-grade classroom. Perhaps it is that, during every professional learning community meeting, there should be an explicit examination of individual and classroom level data and a consideration of alternative teaching strategies that could improve student results. Keep it simple, with an expectation that is so clear, so explicit, and so consistent that you have a very high degree of confidence that you will find uniform results. Then make some systematic observations. At 9:30 a.m., go to five different second-grade classrooms, and see if your observations reveal the uniformity of practice you expected. Visit five professional learning community meetings, and simply count the frequency of those that met the expectation of data analysis and evaluation of teaching strategies that you expected. One of the most persistent and important findings reported by a range of researchers, including Gerald Bracey (2005), Michael Schmoker (2005, 2006), William Sanders (1998), Linda Darling-Hammond and Gary Sykes (1999), and many others, is that the most significant variation is not from one school system to another or even one school to another, but from one classroom to another.

Kim Marshall (2009), in the important book *Rethinking Teacher Supervision and Evaluation*, offers specific tools for observing similarities and differences in teaching practice. The application of Marshall's tools will reveal, in many cases, striking differences in daily classroom practice. Sometimes those differences may be due to different levels of professional knowledge, but in the vast majority of cases, differences in teaching and leadership are reflections of personal decisions. "That's just the way I do things," teachers and administrators explain.

Therefore, the resolution of differences is not a matter of rhetoric, evidence, professional learning, or stern administrative warnings. Rather, leaders must identify which differences of opinion and practice are worthy of the emotional and leadership energy required to resolve them. The three-level decision-making typology is a good way to start. First, identify the type 1 decisions, where teachers have discretion. Second, identify those type 2 decisions where the final result is a collaborative effort by teachers and administrators. Third, identify the type 3 decisions that genuinely represent the factors that influence the safety of students and the values of the educational system.

A great deal of what happens in the classroom is a type 1 decision, a matter of minute-to-minute discretion by the teacher. Type 2 decisions include those that depend upon the collaborative efforts of teachers, such as the common formative assessments that they periodically provide for all students. Type 3 decisions should be limited to matters that are of the highest importance, those issues where leaders must exercise their authority to ensure the welfare of students. For example, safety issues such as crossing guards, cafeteria hygiene, and playground equipment are not matters of individual taste but of system-level policy. We can make the case that reducing student failure through the removal of ineffective grading policies is also a safety issue, because students who fail academically and ultimately drop out of school suffer risks that adversely influence their health and the economic viability of the nation (Alliance for Excellent Education, 2010).

Grading Policies for Special Education Students

In a growing number of nations, there are specific protections for the rights of exceptional students. In general, schools provide for adaptations and accommodations for these students. When a student in a wheelchair cannot reach the lab surface in the science room or the dictionary stand in the library, the accommodations required are straightforward. In physical education classes, the same wheelchair-bound student can engage actively in strategy, competition, cardiovascular exercise, and virtually every class activity. Indeed, as the

Paralympics movement has demonstrated, there is no contradiction in the term "wheelchair athlete." However, the issue of adaptation and accommodation becomes considerably more complex when schools attempt to use traditional grading systems for students with a wide range of physical, neurological, and emotional challenges.

The best guidance for schools on the application of grading to students with special needs is based on the principles with which we began this book: grades must be accurate, fair, specific, and timely.

Accuracy

In some nations, such as the United States, there is a specific requirement in federal legislation that students with disabilities must receive an individualized education plan (IEP) that specifies the modifications, adaptations, and instructional strategies to be used for the student. Therefore, the most accurate way to grade students using an IEP is to use the IEP itself as the frame of reference for the report card. If, for example, Michelle's IEP specifies eight reading objectives, an accurate report card might include the information that she fully achieved four of those objectives, partially achieved two of them, and did not achieve two. The report card would then explain the steps that were being taken collaboratively by Michelle's instructional team to create appropriate instructional modifications and further appropriate adaptations so that she will continue this pursuit of standards. Note that, even though Michelle did not achieve every objective, the process was not unsuccessful. The process was accurate and therefore allowed both the student and her teachers to make midcourse corrections to improve her education. Think of how much more helpful such a process is than the common statement, "Because Michelle had an IEP, I gave her a B in English," even though the student, teacher, and parents all know that Michelle's grade of B was based on work that was not close to the work performed by other students who received the same grade. When the law requires that students receive individualized curriculum and assessment, the use of letter or numerical grades—perhaps the ultimate in standardized and nonindividualized assessment—seems unwise.

Fairness

In the context of special education students, accuracy and fairness are inextricably linked. The demand for accuracy in assessing writing, for example, implies that we focus our assessment on the quality of student writing, not the speed of writing; our assessment of the quality of mathematical prowess is not the same as an assessment of the speed of mathematical calculation. This distinction is the reason that one of the most important adaptations for special education students is the availability of more time to complete the task at hand. Rather than lower the expectation of the teacher, so that a poor job is done in haste, the adaptation of time conveys the essential expectation that students can perform at high levels. The consequence for their failure to do so is neither sympathy from the teacher nor a compensatory grade ("She's in special education, so I had to give her a B") but rather the most appropriate adaptation of all—time. In my own teaching career, I have worked with students who proceeded from fragmentary sentences to sequential lists to complete sentences to paragraphs to essays. Sometimes this process required three months; sometimes it took three years. I am not naïve about the profound difficulty faced by students with learning disabilities, but neither am I dismayed nor intimidated by the fact that it takes some students longer to process information and produce results than other students.

Specificity

Special education teachers are masters of "incrementalization," the process of taking a task that might have seemed to many classroom teachers as a single unit of work and breaking it down into its essential components. This is, in fact, not merely a special education technique but the essence of what outstanding coaches, teachers, executives, and performance analysts do at every level in every field. However, special education teachers bring a consistency and discipline to the process of incrementalization that is particularly useful in a discussion of effective grading practices. Rather than evaluating a single skill, such as reading comprehension, a special educator might consider enumerating the steps that Michelle has learned in order to improve her reading comprehension. These might include:

- Prereading—finding topic sentences and gaining an initial understanding of the author's purpose

- Highlighting unfamiliar words—reducing frustration in reading the passage by identifying, in advance, which words may require definition or an attempt to understand them in context

- Building an idea organizer—visually demonstrating the relationships between facts and conclusions, causes and effects, or claims and counterclaims

- Summarizing—restating the text in her own words and checking for understanding

In fact, Michelle can read and understand challenging grade-level material, but sometimes she never finishes reading that material if she does not follow this very disciplined process to approach the text. It is not helpful for Michelle or her parents if a report card says, "Reading: C minus." She may simply conclude, "See, I knew I was a bad reader." However, if the feedback is specific, Michelle will then have a report card that provides feedback that can lead to better achievement. "Michelle is superior when it comes to prereading and highlighting unfamiliar words. Now she needs to practice more on building idea organizers from texts. In particular, she needs to work on the following types of text: identifying causes and effects." It is worth noting that these same techniques are used not only for effective interventions to help struggling readers but also by advanced students studying medicine, law, history, and other graduate-level disciplines.

Timeliness

Although feedback can have a powerful impact on student learning, the power of feedback is directly related to the timeliness with which it is provided. Because of the legal burdens associated with the documentation of meetings for special education teams, we should acknowledge that while these teams can set long-term strategy for students, they are not the right venue for providing timely feedback to improve student performance. That remains the province of the classroom and special education teachers. Therefore, it is particularly important that the daily feedback provided to students is exceptionally clear in purpose and that this feedback is evaluated in terms of its results.

If, for example, a student who is unable to concentrate for extended periods of time is confronted with thirty prealgebra problems as a fifth-grade homework assignment, one common adaptation might be to reduce the number of problems. This is a perfectly logical solution if and only if the reduced number of problems will allow the student to nevertheless gain sufficient practice to understand the grade-level material. Of course, if a student with an IEP can gain sufficient practice with fifteen, rather than thirty, problems, then so can the rest of the class. It is possible, however, that the mere quantity of problems is not really addressing the problem.

For Max, another student in Michelle's class, the following problem might as well be in Sanskrit: "Find the y-intercept, where $y = mx + b$ and the slope is 2.5 . . ." Max never got past the word *intercept*. Just as with Michelle's series of paragraphs, this problem is a multipiece puzzle that must be broken down into its component parts. Perhaps Max's teacher will work on a series of steps for each problem, including finding the question, having students list the variables they know, the variables they don't know, and so on. In other words, having fifteen impenetrable problems rather than thirty is not the solution to the challenge Max is facing. Receiving a report card that says, "Math: B+ with adaptations" is equally unhelpful. Max really does need to understand this problem, as it is the basis for many other things he will do in geometry, algebra, and statistics in future years. His success in pursuing this objective, however, will require much more from him and his teachers than simply turning in a series of shortened assignments. The grading system for Max will serve him best if teachers do not attempt to use an ill-fitting standard report card with letters and numbers.

The challenge for Max and for every student is to understand with clarity and specificity what he can do, what he needs to work on, and what the best strategies are for his next steps in learning.

LEADING CHANGE IN GRADING SYSTEMS

The acid test for any grading system, whether or not for exceptional students, is the degree to which it is working. By "working," I mean whether students, teachers, and parents can use the feedback from the grading system to improve performance. Students in the early primary grades can, when given the opportunity, respond to the question, "What do you think you need to do to get better?" Those whose teachers have employed standards-based assessment systems in student-accessible language can say with confidence, "I only got a 2, because I forgot to . . ." and quickly add, "but next time I'm going to get a 3 because I will . . ." The use of numbers, letters, or words is immaterial in this example. What is most important, when evaluating grading systems against the standard of effectiveness, is that students use the feedback to improve their performance.

While almost all schools have discussed reforms in grading systems, those that succeed in implementing change effectively follow some distinctive and consistent patterns. First, they do not merely announce a change in grading policy but engage in an extensive community dialogue. School leaders from Waukesha, Wisconsin to Wamego, Kansas recently wrote to me describing their careful process of deliberate, deep, and broad engagement of stakeholders, including students, parents, school board members, union leaders, and community members. They documented their own best practices and considered carefully the best available evidence from national and international sources.

Their changes in grading policies, while not universally popular, were the subject of extensive collaboration and dialogue.

Second, leaders of successful changes in grading policies have a clear set of principles about the fundamental purposes of grading as a tool for improved student learning. They reject grading as a form of punishment and manipulation and embrace it as a means of communication and feedback. Their purpose is neither to sort students nor to judge them, but to help them become more successful.

Third, these change leaders are tolerant of dissent, but they are not intimidated by it. They do not expect every conversation to be easy or viewpoints to be unaccompanied by strong emotions. They recognize that existing grading policies have strong advocates, not because those advocates are bad people, but because they care deeply about their profession and practice. Both sides emerge from these difficult conversations because they recognize that people can differ on the issues and nevertheless share a passionate commitment to children.

Fourth and most importantly, school leaders who are changing grading policies are demonstrating the effectiveness of their changes with improved student success. They win over skeptics not with rhetoric but with results. When their grading policies improve, their failure rates decline. When failures decline, discipline and morale improve. When fewer resources are diverted to course repetition and student remediation, more resources are available for activities that engage the interest and excitement of students and teachers alike. Ultimately, their actions are not based on authority or policy, but on impact.

Appendix

REPRODUCIBLES

Distortions in Grading Through Use of Zero

Use these graphs to understand how distortions in grading arise by using the zero for missing work. Mark the point value for missing work on each graph, and look at the relative weight of the grade in each case.

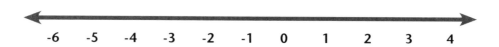

Equity in Grading Self-Assessment

The purpose of this form is to help teachers and administrators explore the relationship between student grades, academic performance, and nonacademic factors. This inquiry may be helpful in improving the equity of your assessment and grading practices. Although designed for classroom use, it can be modified for use by an entire school or school system.

1. Treasure Hunt: Find the A's

Look at the most recent report cards, and enter in the table the names and profiles of students who earned A's or, if you use a different terminology for reporting student results, the highest available mark.

Name	Gender	Low Income?	Ethnic Minority?	Language Minority?

What do you notice about the profile of your A students? What demographic characteristics do they have in common?

2. Search and Rescue Mission: Find the D's and F's

Look at the most recent report cards, and enter in the table the names and profiles of students who earned D's and F's or, if you use a different terminology for reporting student results, the lowest available marks.

Name	Gender	Low Income?	Ethnic Minority?	Language Minority?

What do you notice about the profile of your lowest-performing students? What demographic characteristics do they have in common?

3. High Grades and Low Achievement

Look at your most recent external assessment data. These might be state or provincial tests, district tests, or any other indicator outside of regular classroom work. Find the students who were not proficient on these tests but had good grades in your class—B's and A's or comparable marks in a nonletter grading system—and record their profiles.

Name	Gender	Low Income?	Ethnic Minority?	Language Minority?

What do you notice about the profile of your students with high grades and low achievement? What demographic characteristics do they have in common?

4. Low Grades and High Achievement

Refer to your most recent external assessments, and find the students who scored well but nevertheless have low grades—D's and F's or comparable marks in your system.

Name	Gender	Low Income?	Ethnic Minority?	Language Minority?

What do you notice about the profiles of your students with high achievement and low grades? What demographic characteristics do they have in common?

REFERENCES

Ainsworth, L. (2003). *Power standards: Identifying the standards that matter the most.* Englewood, CO: Advanced Learning Press.

Ainsworth, L., & Christinson, J. (1998). *Student-generated rubrics: An assessment model to help all students succeed.* Orangeburg, NY: Seymour.

Alliance for Excellent Education. (2010, June 9). *The economic benefits of reducing the dropout rate in the nation's largest metropolitan areas.* Accessed at www.al14ed.org/publication_material/EconMSA on June 10, 2010.

American Academy of Pediatrics, Committee on School Health. (2000). Corporal punishment in schools. *Pediatrics, 106*(2), 343.

Amnesty International. (2008). *Amnesty International report 2008: The state of the world's human rights.* London: Author. Accessed at www.amnesty.org/en/library/asset/POL10/001/2008/en/d7c5dcf0-aadd-4eba-9080-10c216523e3a/p01100012008eng.pdf on February 28, 2010.

Bracey, G. (2005). Tips for readers of research: How mean is the median? *Phi Delta Kappan, 87*(1), 92–93.

Calkins, L. M. (1983). *Lessons from a child: On the teaching and learning of writing.* Portsmouth, NH: Heinemann.

Calkins, L. M. (1994). *The art of teaching writing* (2nd ed.). Portsmouth, NH: Heinemann.

Campbell, D. T., & Stanley, J. C. (1963). *Experimental and quasi-experimental designs for research.* Chicago: Rand McNally.

City, E. A., Elmore, R. F., Fiarman, S. E., & Teitel, L. (2009). *Instructional rounds in education: A network approach to improving teaching and learning.* Cambridge, MA: Harvard Education Press.

Clymer, J. B., & Wiliam, D. (2006/2007). Improving the way we grade science. *Educational Leadership, 64*(4), 36–42.

Colvin, G. (2008). *Talent is overrated: What really separates world-class performers from everybody else.* New York: Portfolio.

Darling-Hammond, L. (2010). *The flat world and education: How America's commitment to equity will determine our future.* New York: Teachers College Press.

Darling-Hammond, L. D., & Sykes, G. (1999). *Teaching as the learning profession: Handbook of policy and practice.* San Francisco: Jossey-Bass.

Deutschman, A. (2007). *Change or die: The three keys to change at work and in life.* New York: HarperCollins.

Duckworth, A. L., Peterson, C., Matthews, M. D., & Kelly, D. R. (2007). Grit: Perseverance and passion for long-term goals. *Journal of Personality and Social Psychology, 92*(6), 1087–1101.

DuFour, R., DuFour, R., & Eaker, R. (2008). *Revisiting professional learning communities at work: New insights for improving schools.* Bloomington, IN: Solution Tree Press.

DuFour, R., & Marzano, R. J. (2009). High-leverage strategies for principal leadership. *Educational Leadership, 66*(5), 62–69.

Dweck, C. S. (2006). *Mindset: The new psychology of success.* New York: Random House.

Ericcson, K. A., Charness, N., Hoffman, R. R., & Feltovich, P. J. (Eds.). (2006). *The Cambridge handbook of expertise and expert performance.* New York: Cambridge University Press.

Fullan, M. (2008a). *The six secrets of change: What the best leaders do to help their organizations survive and thrive.* San Francisco: Jossey-Bass.

Fullan, M. (2008b). *What's worth fighting for in the principalship?* (2nd ed.). New York: Teachers College Press.

Fullan, M. (2010). *All systems go: The change imperative for whole system reform.* Thousand Oaks, CA: Corwin Press.

Gallagher, W. (2009). *Rapt: Attention and the focused life.* New York: Penguin.

Gawande, A. (2009). *The checklist manifesto: How to get things right.* New York: Metropolitan Books.

Gladwell, M. (2008). *Outliers: The story of success.* New York: Little, Brown and Company.

Gladwell, M. (2009). *What the dog saw: And other adventures.* New York: Little, Brown and Company.

Guskey, T. R. (2000). Grading policies that work against standards . . . and how to fix them. *NASSP Bulletin, 84*(620), 20–29.

Guskey, T. R. (Ed.). (2009). *The teacher as assessment leader.* Bloomington, IN: Solution Tree Press.

Guskey, T. R., & Bailey, J. M. (2001). *Developing grading and reporting systems for student learning.* Thousand Oaks, CA: Corwin Press.

Hattie, J. (2009). *Visible learning: A synthesis of over 800 meta-analyses relating to achievement.* New York: Routledge.

Heath, C., & Heath, D. (2010). *Switch: How to change things when change is hard.* New York: Broadway Books.

Hensley, D., & Carlin, D. (2005). *Mastering competitive debate* (7th ed.). Logan, IA: Perfection Learning.

Herrnstein, R. J., & Murray, C. (1994). *The bell curve: Intelligence and class structure in American life.* New York: Free Press.

Human Rights Watch. (2008, August). *A violent education: Corporal punishment of children in U.S. public schools.* Accessed at www.aclu.org/pdfs/humanrights/aviolenteducation_report.pdf on February 26, 2010.

Ingersoll, R., & Perda, D. (2009). *How high is teacher turnover and is it a problem?* Madison, WI: Consortium for Policy Research in Education.

Kafer, K. (2005, March 1). U.S. girl students outperform boys in most subjects, study finds. *School Reform News.* Accessed at www.heartland.org/policybot/results/16492/US_Girl_Students_Outperform_Boys_in_Most_Subjects_Study_Finds.html on June 10, 2010.

Kim, W. C., & Mauborgne, R. (2003, January). Fair process: Managing in the knowledge economy. *Harvard Business Review Online.* Accessed at http://hbr.org/2003/01/fair-process/ar/1 on March 15, 2010.

Kohn, A. (1999). *Punished by rewards: The trouble with gold stars, incentive plans, A's, praise, and other bribes.* Boston: Houghton Mifflin.

Kotter, J. P. (1996). *Leading change.* Boston: Harvard Business School Press.

Kotter, J. P. (2008). *A sense of urgency.* Boston: Harvard Business School Press.

Lehrer, J. (2009). *How we decide.* New York: Houghton Mifflin.

Lemov, D. (2010). *Teach like a champion: 49 techniques that put students on the path to college.* San Francisco: Jossey-Bass.

Marsh, H. W. (1984). Students' evaluations of university teaching: Dimensionality, reliability, validity, potential biases and utility. *Journal of Educational Psychology, 76,* 707–754.

Marshall, K. (2009). *Rethinking teacher supervision and evaluation: How to work smart, build collaboration, and close the achievement gap.* San Francisco: Jossey-Bass.

Marzano, R. J. (2007). *The art and science of teaching: A comprehensive framework for effective instruction.* Alexandria, VA: Association for Supervision and Curriculum Development.

Marzano, R. J. (2009). *Designing & teaching learning goals & objectives.* Bloomington, IN: Marzano Research Laboratory.

Marzano, R. J. (Ed.). (2010). *On excellence in teaching.* Bloomington, IN: Solution Tree Press.

Marzano, R. J., & Kendall, J. S. (1998). *Implementing standards-based education.* Washington, DC: National Education Association.

McAfee, A. (2009, November 20). *It's time to embrace evidence-based medicine.* Accessed at http://blogs.harvardbusiness.org/hbr/mcafee/2009/11/its-time-to-embrace-evidenceba.html on December 20, 2009.

O'Connor, K. (2007). *A repair kit for grading: 15 fixes for broken grades.* Portland, OR: Educational Testing Service.

O'Connor, K. (2009). *How to grade for learning K–12* (3rd ed.). Thousand Oaks, CA: Corwin Press.

Patterson, K., Grenny, J., Maxfield, D., McMillan, R., & Switzler, A. (2008). *Influencer: The power to change anything.* New York: McGraw-Hill.

Pfeffer, J., & Sutton, R. I. (2006a). Evidence-based management. *Harvard Business Review, 84*(1), 62–74.

Pfeffer, J., & Sutton, R. I. (2006b). *Hard facts, dangerous half-truths and total nonsense: Profiting from evidence-based management.* Boston: Harvard Business School Press.

Pink, D. H. (2009). *Drive: The surprising truth about what motivates us.* New York: Riverhead Books.

Pogrow, S. (2009). *Teaching content outrageously: How to captivate all students and accelerate learning, grades 4–12.* San Francisco: Jossey-Bass.

Popham, W. J. (2008). *Transformative assessment.* Alexandria, VA: Association for Supervision and Curriculum Development.

Reeves, D. B. (2004). *Accountability for learning: How teachers and school leaders can take charge.* Alexandria, VA: Association for Supervision and Curriculum Development.

Reeves, D. B. (2006a). *The learning leader: How to focus school improvement for better results.* Alexandria, VA: Association for Supervision and Curriculum Development.

Reeves, D. B. (2006b). Preventing 1,000 failures. *Educational Leadership, 64*(3), 88–89.

Reeves, D. B. (2008a). Effective grading practices. *Educational Leadership, 65*(5), 85–87.

Reeves, D. B. (2008b). *Reframing teacher leadership to improve your school.* Alexandria, VA: Association for Supervision and Curriculum Development.

Reeves, D. B. (2009a). *Assessing educational leaders: Evaluating performance for improved individual and organizational results* (2nd ed.). Thousand Oaks, CA: Corwin Press.

Reeves, D. B. (2009b). *Leading change in your school: How to conquer myths, build commitment, and get results.* Alexandria, VA: Association for Supervision and Curriculum Development.

Reeves, D. B. (2009c). Remaking the grade, from A to D. *Chronicle of Higher Education.* Accessed at http://chronicle.com/article/Remaking-the-Grade-From-A-to/48352/ on March 15, 2010.

Rosenthal, R., & DiMatteo, M. R. (2001). Meta-analysis: Recent developments in quantitative methods for literature reviews. *Annual Review of Psychology, 52,* 59–82.

Sanders, W. L. (1998, December). Value added assessments. *School Administrator.* Accessed at www.aasa.org/publications/saarticledetail.cfm?ItemNumber=4627 on November 17, 2006.

Schmoker, M. (2005). No turning back: The ironclad case for professional learning communities. In R. DuFour, R. Eaker, & R. DuFour (Eds.), *On common ground: The power of professional learning communities* (pp. 135–153). Bloomington, IN: Solution Tree Press.

Schmoker, M. (2006). *Results now: How we can achieve unprecedented improvements in teaching and learning.* Alexandria, VA: Association for Supervision and Curriculum Development.

Stober, D. R., & Grant, A. M. (Eds.). (2006). *Evidence based coaching handbook: Putting best practices to work for your client.* Hoboken, NJ: Wiley.

Wiggins, G. (1998). *Educative assessment: Designing assessments to inform and improve student performance.* San Francisco: Jossey-Bass.

Willingham, D. T. (2009). *Why don't students like school? A cognitive scientist answers questions about how the mind works and what it means for the classroom.* San Francisco: Jossey-Bass.

INDEX

Ahead of the Curve: The Power of Assessment to Transform Teaching and Learning
Edited by Douglas Reeves
Leaders in education contribute their perspectives of effective assessment design and implementation, sending out a call for redirecting assessment to improve student achievement and inform instruction. **BKF232**

Formative Assessment & Standards-Based Grading
Robert J. Marzano
Learn everything you need to know to implement an integrated system of assessment and grading. Dr. Marzano explains how to design, interpret, and systematically use three different types of formative assessments and how to track student progress and assign meaningful grades. **BKL003**

Balanced Assessment: From Formative to Summative
Kay Burke
This book aids teachers in learning how to integrate formative and summative assessments seamlessly into instruction. Research, strategies, and examples help teachers monitor, grade, and gauge student ability to meet standards. **BKF272**

21st Century Skills: Rethinking How Students Learn
Edited by James Bellanca and Ron Brandt
Education luminaries reveal why 21st century skills are necessary, which skills are most important, and how to help schools include them in curriculum and instruction. **BKF389**